Joomla! with Flash

Build stunning, content-rich, and interactive websites
with Joomla! 1.5 and Flash CS4.

Suhreed Sarkar

BIRMINGHAM - MUMBAI

Joomla! with Flash

First published: November 2009

Production Reference: 1231009

Published by Packt Publishing Ltd.
32 Lincoln Road
Olton
Birmingham, B27 6PA, UK.

ISBN 978-1-847198-24-2

www.packtpub.com

Cover Image by Vinayak Chittar (vinayak.chittar@gmail.com)

Credits

Author
Suhreed Sarkar

Reviewers
Jose Argudo
Sonia Muñoz

Acquisition Editor
Usha Iyer

Development Editor
Swapna Verlekar

Technical Editor
Kartik Thakkar

Copy Editor
Leonard D'Silva

Editorial Team Leader
Akshara Aware

Project Coordinator
Srimoyee Ghoshal

Indexers
Monica Ajmera
Hemangini Bari

Proofreaders
Kevin McGowan
Chris Smith

Production Coordinator
Adline Swetha Jesuthas

Cover Work
Adline Swetha Jesuthas

About the Author

Suhreed Sarkar — an IT consultant, a trainer, and a technical writer — after completing Marine engineering, he served on board a ship for two years and then started his journey into the world of IT with an MCSE in Windows NT 4.0 track. Later, he studied business administration and earned an MBA from the University of Dhaka. He has a bunch of BrainBench certifications on various topics including PHP4, Project Management, RDBMS Concepts, E-Commerce, Web Server Administration, Internet Security, Training Development, Training Delivery and Evaluation, and Technical Writing.

As a trainer, he has taught courses on system administration, web development, e-commerce, and MIS. He has consulted for several national and international organizations including the United Nations and has helped clients in building and adopting their web portals, large scale databases, and management information systems. At present, he is working on building a framework for the education sector MIS and is promoting the use of ICTs in education.

Suhreed is a renowned technical author in Bengali having dozens of books published on subjects covering web development, LAMP, networking, and system administration. He authored the *Zen Cart: E-commerce Application Development*, and *Joomla! E-commerce with VirtueMart* books. Both of them are published by Packt Publishing.

While not busy with hacking some apps, blogging on his blog (www.suhreedsarkar. com), reading the philosophy of Bertrand Russell or management thoughts of Peter F. Drucker, he likes to spend some special moments with his family. Suhreed lives in Dhaka, Bangladesh.

Acknowledgement

Firstly, I am grateful to the Joomla! community and the developers and maintainers of the extensions discussed in this book, as without them, the book could not have been written.

I would like to thank the Packt team for their excellent professional support, and a special thanks to Usha Iyer, Swapna Verleker, Srimoyee Ghoshal, and Kartik Thakkar who have helped me throughout the whole process. I express my heartiest gratitude to the reviewers for providing their insightful comments on the first draft of this book. I thank my family and friends for being patient while I was working on this book.

About the Reviewers

Jose Argudo is a web developer from Valencia, Spain. After finishing his studies, he started working for a web designing company. After six years of working for that company and others, he decided to start working as a freelancer.

Now, after some years have passed, he thinks that it's the best decision he has ever made, a decision that lets him work with the tools he likes, such as Joomla!, CodeIgniter, CakePHP, JQuery, and other well-known open source technologies.

For the last few months, he has also been reviewing some of the books for Packt Publishing, such as *Magento 1.3 Theme Design*, *Magento: Beginner's Guide*, *Magento Development with PHP*, *Joomla! SEO*, and *Symfony 1.3 Web Application Development*.

If that weren't enough, he is also writing a book on CodeIgniter for Packt Publishing—a book he is putting all his efforts on.

To Silvia and Luis.

Sonia Muñoz is a web developer from Spain. She has completed the Superior Computer Systems Management course and is now willing to start with another of Superior Development's computer application courses. She has worked with tools like PHP, MySQL, HTML, CSS, jQuery, JavaScript, CodeIgniter, Joomla, Photoshop, and Dreamweaver.

After finishing her studies, she would like to set up her own web development business.

I dedicate this book to my father-in-law, Abul Hossain

Table of Contents

Preface

Joomla! is an award winning Content Management System with lots of features. It is useful for almost all types of websites. It has an object-oriented, modular architecture with lots of extensibility features. You can build almost any kind of a website using Joomla!. It has a strong security, authentication, and authorization framework, a content management framework, and a templating system.

There are thousands of Joomla! components, modules, and plugins to extend the functionality of Joomla!. A component for Joomla! can be compared to an application for Joomla!. Similarly, modules are extensions to display the data on Joomla!-based websites. Plugins are also extensions for performing special tasks, such as pre- and post-filtering of content for Joomla!-based websites. With all these features of Joomla! that provide ease of administration and options for customization, sometimes you may think of integrating other technologies, such as Flash, into it. This is because Flash provides great features for animation, which is otherwise not possible using only Joomla!, HTML, or JavaScript.

Flash is unique in creating animated objects, and this adds an extra flavor to your Joomla!-based website. Besides stunning graphics, design, and layout, Flash can definitely add interactivity and value to the website. Some of the features, such as animations, small videos, and interactive games, are only possible through Flash. Considering these unique features of Flash, Joomla! developers have long been trying to use Flash content in Joomla! websites. This book shows you how to use Flash objects with Joomla! content with minimal efforts and maximum output.

What this book covers

Chapter 1: Get Started with Flash in Joomla! begins with a discussion on why one should opt for using Flash in Joomla! and what are the benefits of doing this. Next, it introduces us to the different types of Flash objects and various tools that will be useful for developing Flash and Joomla!-based sites.

Chapter 2: Enhance Your Joomla! Content with Flash teaches us how to use Flash-based image slideshows in our Joomla! website and display them at different module positions. As the chapter progresses, we learn to embed Flash animations into articles and finally learn to embed Flash movies at different module positions and within articles.

Chapter 3: Creating Attractive Menus with Flash begins with an introduction to the built-in menu system of Joomla!. It then illustrates the use of two extensions, Flash Floating Menu and Super Web Flash module for Joomla! 1.5, for embedding Flash-based menus into our Joomla! website and also lists a few other extensions.

In *Chapter 4: Creating Flash Photo Galleries*, we are introduced to the concept of building Flash photo galleries for our Joomla!-based website. This chapter begins with an illustration of the Expose Flash Gallery component and proceeds to the use of the Expose Scroller module and the Expose plugin. Next, we learn to embed a 3D Flash-based photo galley in our website with the help of Ozio Gallery. We also learn how to embed images from Flickr, as well as from our web server, and which of the skins available with Ozio Gallery can be used for doing so. Finally, we learn to use three simpler extensions for embedding Flash photo galleries—New Gallery, Simple Image Flash Gallery, and Dynamic Flash Gallery.

Chapter 5: Flashier than Ever: Maps, Charts, Custom Fonts, Multimedia, and More extends the use of Flash on our Joomla!-based website. Firstly, we learn to build interactive Flash-based maps and charts using the YOS amMap and amChart components respectively. Then the chapter illustrates the use of sIFR with Joomla! for displaying the contents of a Joomla! site in fonts that are not installed on users' computers. The use of the Joomla! Flash Uploader component is also illustrated. Further, the chapter takes us through how to create streaming video sites with the use of the JVideo! components and discusses various extensions for adding an MP3 player on your Joomla! website.

Chapter 6: Flash Decorations: Flashy Templates, Headers, Banners, and Tickers deals with using Flash templates for decorating our website with Flash logos, headers, banners, and tickers. In this chapter, we are introduced to the two ways of showing Flash objects in a Joomla! site, namely, by embedding the Flash object in a Joomla! template showing it permanently on a Joomla! website and by using a suitable module. Furthermore, the use of Joomla! modules like FlexHeader3 and Web Flash Joomla! for displaying Flash objects is also discussed in this chapter.

Chapter 7: Playing with Code focuses mainly on the issue of how we embed Joomla! content into a Flash site, which is exactly the opposite of what has been done in the previous chapters, using the J-AMFPHP component. In this chapter, we also take a look at some of the accessibility issues and ways to address these issues.

Chapter 8: Troubleshoot Your Applications deals with the most common problems with Joomla!, Flash, and the Joomla! extensions that have been discussed in this book. Besides pointing to the probable solution for such problems, the chapter also provides references to relevant websites and forums that can prove to be helpful in solving problems.

Appendix: Resources for Joomla! and Flash gives you a list of some more resources that can be useful for using Flash with Joomla!. Firstly, it shows some resources for Joomla!, and then it lists some Flash extension-specific resources.

What you need for this book

First of all, you will need the Apache-MySQL-PHP environment for running Joomla!. For this book, we have used Joomla! 1.5.14. All the descriptions and screenshots are based on this version of Joomla!. If you do not have access to any web-hosting service, then you still can use Joomla! and learn about it on your own computer. In that case, you need to set up the development environment by installing WAMP on your Windows machine. Further information on setting up the development environment on your Windows computer is provided in Chapter 1. To get the exact results, this book should be followed from the beginning to the end, and you should perform the tasks as described.

It is assumed that readers of this book have knowledge on Joomla! and a basic knowledge of Flash. Besides knowledge on the Apache-MySQL-PHP environment, Joomla!, and Flash, familiarity with HTML, CSS, and PHP will be an added advantage.

Who this book is for

If you are a Joomla! web developer and want to integrate Flash into your websites, then this book is for you!

Conventions

In this book, you will find a number of styles of text that distinguish between different kinds of information. Here are some examples of these styles, and an explanation of their meaning.

Code words in text are shown as follows: " As you can see, the <object> </object> tag can contain child elements."

A block of code is set as follows:

```
{yos_amchart chartid='4' width='500' height='500' flashv='8'
  bgcolour='#ffffc0' plugin='1'}
```

When we wish to draw your attention to a particular part of a code block, the relevant lines or items are set in bold:

```
<positions>
    <position>flexheader</position>
    <position>left</position>
    <position>user1</position>
    ...
    <position>right</position>
    <position>debug</position>
</positions>
```

New terms and **important words** are shown in bold. Words that you see on the screen, in menus or dialog boxes for example, appear in the text like this: " Once downloaded and installed, you will find the module in the **Extensions | Module Manager** screen."

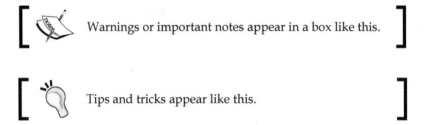

Warnings or important notes appear in a box like this.

Tips and tricks appear like this.

Reader feedback

Feedback from our readers is always welcome. Let us know what you think about this book — what you liked or may have disliked. Reader feedback is important for us to develop titles that you really get the most out of.

To send us general feedback, simply send an email to feedback@packtpub.com, and mention the book title via the subject of your message.

If there is a book that you need and would like to see us publish, please send us a note in the **SUGGEST A TITLE** form on www.packtpub.com or email suggest@packtpub.com.

If there is a topic that you have expertise in and you are interested in either writing or contributing to a book, see our author guide on www.packtpub.com/authors.

Customer support

Now that you are the proud owner of a Packt book, we have a number of things to help you to get the most from your purchase.

Errata

Although we have taken every care to ensure the accuracy of our content, mistakes do happen. If you find a mistake in one of our books—maybe a mistake in the text or the code—we would be grateful if you would report this to us. By doing so, you can save other readers from frustration, and help us to improve subsequent versions of this book. If you find any errata, please report them by visiting http://www.packtpub. com/support, selecting your book, clicking on the **let us know** link, and entering the details of your errata. Once your errata are verified, your submission will be accepted and the errata added to any list of existing errata. Any existing errata can be viewed by selecting your title from http://www.packtpub.com/support.

Piracy

Piracy of copyright material on the Internet is an ongoing problem across all media. At Packt, we take the protection of our copyright and licenses very seriously. If you come across any illegal copies of our works, in any form, on the Internet, please provide us with the location address or website name immediately so that we can pursue a remedy.

Please contact us at copyright@packtpub.com with a link to the suspected pirated material.

We appreciate your help in protecting our authors, and our ability to bring you valuable content.

Questions

You can contact us at questions@packtpub.com if you are having a problem with any aspect of the book, and we will do our best to address it.

1
Get Started with Flash in Joomla!

We assume that you know what Joomla! and Flash are. You have taken this title because you want to build stunning websites with Joomla! and Flash. The only thing you may need to know is how to use Flash with the powerful Joomla! **Content Management System (CMS)** and build a Joomla!-based website with stunning Flash animations. With this assumption, we proceed to building websites with Joomla! and Flash, without delving into what Joomla! and Flash are.

Before starting with the techniques of building stunning websites with Joomla! and Flash, some of you may be interested in knowing the reasons for using Flash in Joomla!, and also may be interested in knowing how to create Flash objects. In this chapter, we will discuss about:

- Why use Flash in Joomla! CMS
- How to create Flash objects
- Some useful tools for working with Flash objects

On the completion of this chapter, you will be able to select the appropriate tools required for working with Flash objects.

Why use Flash in Joomla!?

There is no doubt that Joomla! is a very powerful CMS. It has an object-oriented, modular architecture with lots of extensibility features. Joomla! is feature-rich and useful for almost all types of websites. You can build almost any kind of website using Joomla!. It has a strong security, authentication and authorization framework, content management framework, and templating system. The look and feel of a Joomla! website can largely be customized through its templates. There are thousands of templates available for Joomla!, many of which are very visually pleasing.

In addition to templates, there are also thousands of Joomla! components, modules, and plugins. Components, modules, and plugins are ways to extend Joomla!'s functionality. A component for Joomla! can be compared to an application for Joomla!. For example, if you want to add a photo gallery, there are several components that provide this functionality. You may choose any of the Joomla! components and extend the functionality of your Joomla! website. If you want to build an e-commerce site, then you can add an e-commerce component, such as the VirtueMart, and add that functionality to your Joomla!-based website. Similarly, modules are extensions to display the data on Joomla!-based websites. Plugins are also extensions for performing specials tasks, such as pre- and post-filtering of contents, for Joomla!-based websites.

With all these features of Joomla!, ease of administration and options for customization, sometimes you may think of integrating other technologies such as Flash into it. This is because Flash provides great features for animation, which are otherwise not possible using only Joomla!, HTML, or JavaScript. Flash is unique in creating animated objects, and this adds an extra flavor to your Joomla!-based website. For example, suppose you have to create an attractive site for kids. The site aims to provide interactive games, videos, and animations for the kids. It is an edutainment site and should be attractive enough to hold its audience. In addition to stunning graphics, design, and layout, Flash can definitely add value to the website. Some of the features such as animations, small videos, and interactive games, can only be possible through Flash.

Using Flash with Joomla! can benefit you in the following ways:

- You can add streaming videos, animations, and more of such interactive objects inside Joomla! contents or articles. Adding graphical and multimedia objects like these provides a better user experience.
- Besides using the default menu system of Joomla! and some other extensions for making the Joomla! menus more attractive, you can use Flash menus to give the users a better visual experience.
- Joomla! has many components for showing photo galleries. It is widely accepted that Flash-based photo galleries are visually richer than normal galleries built upon HTML, PHP, CSS, and JavaScript. You can add Flash photo galleries to a Joomla! website and make your photo galleries visually rich.
- Besides menus, photo galleries, and videos, you can also use Flash-based charts, graphs, and maps with your Joomla! articles.
- For improving the overall design and the look and feel of your site, you can use Flash headers, banners, templates, and tickers in Joomla!.

Later in this book, we will learn to add these functionalities and make our site look stunning, visually rich, and interactive.

Creating Flash objects

Adobe Flash was previously known as Macromedia Flash. Flash objects are created using Adobe Flash, a software program created by Macromedia and acquired by Adobe, Inc. The latest version of this software is Adobe Flash CS4.

Nowadays, many applications can generate Flash objects. For example, there are converters that can generate a Flash animation from Microsoft PowerPoint. OpenOffice.org Impress can natively save a presentation as a Flash presentation. Therefore Flash objects are not only generated by Adobe Flash. However, for the sake of this book, we will assume that the animation and Flash objects we are talking about have been created using Adobe Flash.

By using Adobe Flash, we can create multiple types of Flash objects including animations and videos. The application generates the following types of Flash files:

Extension	Description
.fla	Files with this extension are Flash files that can be edited by the Adobe Flash application. This is not a compiled file and is not intended for embedding in to web pages.
.swf	These files are complete and compiled Flash files ready for embedding into web pages. **SWF** means **ShockWave Flash,** and this is the most, format for distributing animated vector graphics. SWF files can be generated using several products, such as Adobe Flash, Adobe Flex, and SWiSH Max 2. There are several other small tools available for creating such animations.
.as	This is a script file generated by ActionScript. Although FLA files can contain scripts directly, for structural purposes separate script files are kept with the extension .as.
.flv	You may be using .flv files already on *YouTube* and other streaming video sites. **FLV** is a **Flash Video** file, ready for streaming with good compression. In fact, Flash video files are container files, which contain the videos and act as wrapper. The file itself is not a video format.
	Flash video files play on most operating systems using Adobe Flash Player and other third party players including VLC Media player, Windows Media Player, RealPlayer, and Media Player Classic. The file format itself is open, but the codecs for this format are proprietary, which makes this format dependent on Adobe Systems.

Adobe Flash Player is available for free at http://www.adobe.com/ products/Flashplayer/. It is required for playing any Flash object embedded in any website.

Some tools for working with Flash

Besides Adobe Flash, there are many other tools currently available for working with Flash objects. Some of these can create Flash objects just as Adobe Flash does. Some are used to create variants of a Flash object, such as a Flash wallpaper, a Flash screensaver, a Flash photo gallery, and so on. In this section, we are going to highlight some of the popular Flash tools that you may need to use while building a Joomla!-based web site with Flash.

SWiSH Max

SWiSH Max is the alternative to Adobe Flash for creating Flash animations, banners, and designs. It has a simpler interface and is often used by users who want a low cost solution for Flash. Many websites are now using SWiSH animations and hundreds of SWiSH templates are available online. For more information and to download a trial version of this stunning Flash designer, visit www.swishzone.com.

The following screenshot shows the designer interface of SWiSH Max:

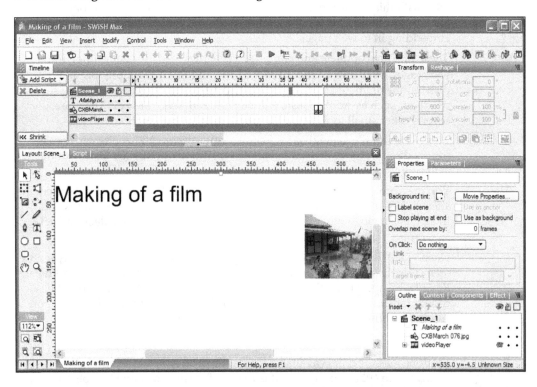

Ajax Animator

Ajax Animator is an online interactive application for building Flash animation. It aims at creating a fully-functional alternative for creating Flash animations. It is available at `http://antimatter15.110mb.com/ajaxanimator/build/`. If you do not have any tool for creating Flash animations, you can use this simple online tool for creating a quick animation with images and text.

The following screenshot shows the interface for the animation builder that can be accessed only by using a web browser:

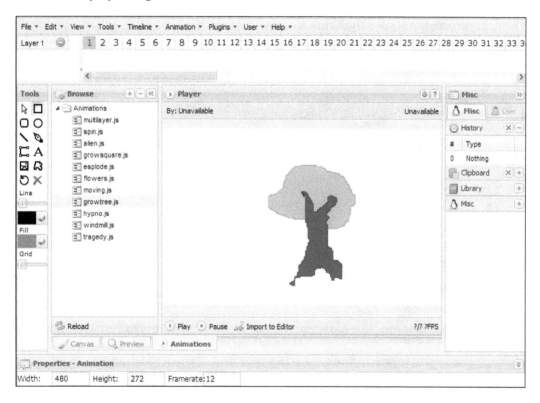

Once created, you can preview the animation and download it to your computer.

Wink

Wink is a freely available software for creating tutorials and demonstrations. The software records screen activities and voices and saves the resulting video as a Flash animation. You can directly upload the Flash animation to a web server and embed it within any web page. A Flash animation created through Wink thus provides an animated learning material with video, captions, and voice. This is best suited for creating software tutorials and presentations, especially when you want to create some teaching/learning materials to demonstrate how to use a software. You can download this software from the website http://www.debugmode.com/wink/.

The next screenshot shows the Wink interface:

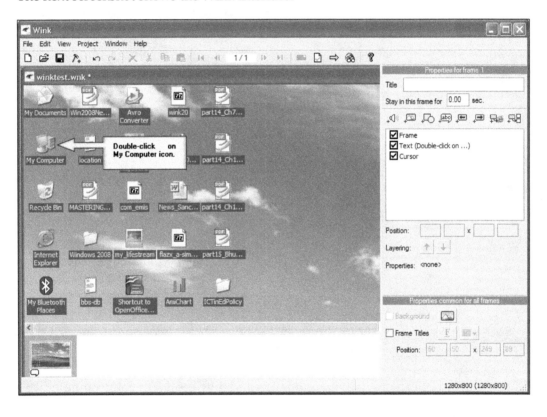

Wink has some other great features too, such as saving the resulting tutorial as an Adobe Flash (SWF) file, a standalone EXE, a PDF, a postscript, and an HTML or any other web image format. It can capture screen activities or use images (BMP, JPG, PNG, TIF, GIF formats) to create a tutorial. The Flash file becomes a highly compressed animation and gives better performance compared to some of the other commercial competing applications. Wink is available for both Windows and Linux operating systems.

When creating a presentation or a tutorial using Wink, you can add callouts, buttons, navigational buttons, and texts through which the users can interact with the tutorial or the presentation.

Flash charting tools

Charting on web pages is a much sought after feature for web developers. At some point, most web developers want to visualize their data in different types of charts. Recently, the Google Visualization API has opened up the door to the use charting and graphing on web pages. However, Flash charting tools still remain popular for the stunning graphs and charts. There are many Flash charting tools that provide ways to create different types of charts. Some of the popular Flash charting tools are described in following sections.

Animated Charts

This proprietary software allows you to create different types of charts from the data you provide. The charts created by this software may have several animations. Dynamic charts can be built using its Pro version. Animated Charts is available from its website `http://www.animatedchart.com/`.

amCharts

amCharts provides the flexibility to generate different types of charts using both static and dynamic data. By default, there are four sets of predefined charts: Pie and Donut, Line and Area, Column and Bar, and Scatter and Bubble. It can dynamically generate 2D as well as 3D Flash charts. amCharts is available for use with Joomla!, and we will be looking at this software in Chapter 5 , *Flashier than Ever: Maps, Charts, Custom Fonts, Multimedia, and More.*

Open Flash Chart

Open Flash Chart is an open source free library of functions that can be used to generate different types of Flash charts. It can be used with different web-scripting languages including PHP, Java, .Net, Perl, Python, and Ruby on Rails. It is feature-rich and easy to use with web-scripting languages. Open Flash Chart is available at http://www.openflashchart.com/. The following screenshot shows a 3D bar chart created using Open Flash Chart:

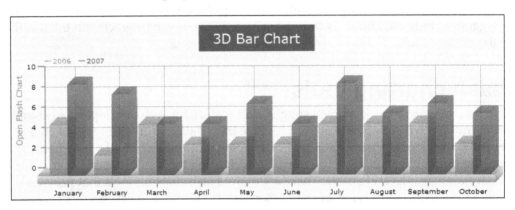

FusionCharts

FusionCharts is a free Flash-charting component that can generate charts from both dynamic as well as static data and can be used with many types of web applications. It is cross-browser and cross-platform and can be used with PHP, ASP, ASP.Net, JSP, ColdFusion, Ruby on Rails, and JSP. You can even use it with simple HTML pages or in PowerPoint presentations. This is a commercial component, but a free version is also available.

By using this component, most of the popular chart formats, including 2D/3D column charts, bar charts, line charts, pie and doughnut charts, stacked charts, and area charts, can be readily generated in an SWF file. The data to be visualized can be taken from XML files. To get a free version of FusionCharts and to know more about it, visit its website at http://www.fusioncharts.com/.

ActionScript libraries

ActionScript is the scripting language for Flash. Most Flash authoring tools now support ActionScript. There are some online repositories from where you can download ActionScript and use these scripts freely. The following are some of the noteworthy ActionScript libraries:

- **Senocular.com ActionScript Library**: This library contains hundreds of scripts for ActionScript versions 1, 2, and 3. The scripts can be browsed and viewed online. You choose a script, copy it, and use it in your Flash object. The library is available at: `http://www.senocular.com/Flash/actionscript.php`.

- **ActionScript.org Library**: This library contains more than 700 scripts that you can use with your Flash animations. It is accessible at `http://www.actionscript.org/actionscripts_library/`.

- **ActionScript Physics Engine**: This is a freely available open source 2D physics engine that can be used with Flash and Flex. It is available at `http://www.cove.org/ape/`.

There are many other sites where you can get lots of ActionScript scripts and tutorials on how to use them.

Riva FLV Encoder

With this encoder you can convert your videos into high-quality Flash Videos (FLV) and embed them into a web page. After selecting a video to transcode into a Flash video, you can use presets or custom settings and later play the converted FLV with the bundled Riva FLV Player. This encoder can transcode AVI, MPEG, QuickTime, and WMV videos into FLV. It can be downloaded free of charge from `http://rivavx.com/?encoder`.

The Riva FLV Encoder is shown in the following screenshot:

sIFR

sIFR is used for adding Flash texts to HTML pages. The font does not need to be installed on the visitor's computer. Instead, by using sIFR, you can create the text in any font as you want, and sIFR will display that text in your desired font irrespective of the availability of the font on the visitor's computer. In Chapter 5, we will be looking into using sIFR in Joomla! sites.

PowerPoint to Flash converter

Many general users may not know how to use Flash. Generating Flash animations may seem difficult to them, or simply, they may not be eager to learn Flash. However, it is expected that most of the readers of this book do know how to make a PowerPoint presentation using text, graphics, and sound. In fact, you can create an animated presentation using PowerPoint, which can later be converted into a Flash object for embedding into your web application. There are many converters which convert a PowerPoint presentation to a Flash animation.

Most of these converters can retain the sound, animation, and other visual effects of PowerPoint presentations. Some are also capable of converting multiple files at once in a batch.

Setting up the development environment

It is always good to set up a development environment and test an application before publishing it on the production web server. For the purpose of this book, we will also set up the development environment with a web server and Joomla!.

Web server

You can use any web server that supports PHP. For the purpose of this book, we will use the most popular web server — Apache, version 1.3 or version 2. If you are using Linux as an operating system, then you may get the Apache server bundled with the Linux OS. However, you are always free to download the latest version of Apache from its website at `http://httpd.apache.org/`. The Apache web server is available for both Linux and Windows operating systems, and you can download the appropriate version for your own operating system.

Database server

In order to use Joomla! we need to set up a relational database system. We will be using MySQL as the database system. Like Apache, MySQL is also available for free to download for Linux, for Windows, and for other platforms as well. You can download it from `http://www.mysql.com/`.

PHP

To run Joomla! we need a web server capable of running PHP scripts. We can easily download the PHP bundle, install it, and configure the Apache web server for PHP. Joomla! will run on both PHP4 and PHP5, but to take advantage of the advanced Joomla! features and PHP5's rich features, we will use PHP5. You can download PHP5 from the website `http://www.php.net`. Like Apache and MySQL, PHP is also available for Linux, Windows, and other platforms.

For the development server, users with less technical skills may find it daunting to set up the web server, database server, and to configure PHP and its libraries. Administration of these services also becomes complex. To ease the task of setting up a development environment with Apache, MySQL, and PHP, there are several packaged software applications, such as WampServer, PHPTriad, EasyPHP, and so on that include all the three services and can be installed in one shot. For our development environment, we will use WampServer for Windows.

The latest version of the WampServer package contains Apache2.2.x, MySQL 5.1.x, and PHP 5.2.x. To setup the development environment for using Joomla! with Flash, follow these steps:

1. **Get the WAMP Server**: The WAMP Server provides you with Apache, MySQL, and PHP. Point your browser to `www.wampserver.com`, and download the latest version of the WAMP Server.

2. **Install the WAMP Server**: Once the WAMP Server is downloaded to your computer, double-click on the installation file. By default, it will be installed at `C:\wamp`. Under that, there will be a directory `www` that is known as the web directory. This means that whatever web application you want to run should be put inside this folder (in our case it is `c:\wamp\www`).

3. **Run the WAMP Server**: You can configure your WAMP Sever to run when Windows starts. Alternatively, you can run it as and when needed. You can start the WAMP Server from **Start | All Programs | WampServer | start WampServer**. When the WAMP Server is started, you will see the WampServer icon in the system tray. Click on that icon, and you get the WampServer menu, as shown in the next screenshot:

For starting all the services (Apache, MySQL, and PHP), click on
Start All Services. For configuring PHP, go to **PHP**. You can create
databases with **phpMyAdmin**.

To see the default page in the web root, click on **Localhost** or type
`http://localhost/` in your browser's address bar. It will display
a page like the one shown in the next screenshot:

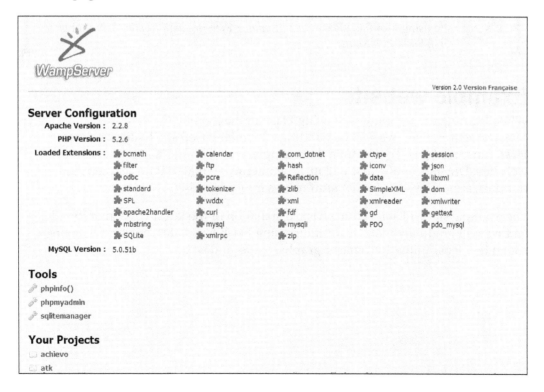

Once you get the web server with MySQL and PHP running, you can proceed with installing Joomla! on that web server as follows:

1. **Get theJoomla installation package**: Now it is your turn to get the Joomla! installation package, through which you will install Joomla! on your local computer. Open your browser and type www.joomla.org in the address bar. You will see the Joomla! home page. On the right side, there is a download link for the latest release. Click on this link to download the latest release of Joomla!. It comes as .zip or .tgz archive.

2. **Create the database for Joomla!:** Before starting the Joomla! installation, you need to create a MySQL database on the localhost. Open your browser and point it to http://localhost/phpmyadmin. In the phpMyAdmin screen, enter the name of the database and create it. Remember the name of the database as the Joomla! installation wizard will ask for it later.

3. **Install Joomla! on your local computer:** Once you have downloaded the installation package for Joomla!, unpack the Joomla! installation files to your web root directory (for example c:\wamp\www\dreamschool), and then point your browser to http://localhost/dreamschool/. That starts the Joomla! installation wizard. Follow the wizard, and complete the Joomla! installation.

 To learn more about Joomla! installation, administration, and building a site using Joomla!, please read *"Building Websites with Joomla! 1.5"*, *Hagen Graf, Packt Publishing*.

Example website

While learning the techniques of using Flash in the Joomla! Content Management System, we will be building a Joomla!-based site to demonstrate Flash functionalities. To illustrate the example, we will build a fictitious school website — DreamSchool — that will include interactive material for learners, video tutorials, animations, and other stuff necessary for learning.

The example site will start with a basic installation of the latest version of Joomla!, and we will gradually make it stunning using Flash templates, headers, banners, content, videos, animation, charts, graphs, maps, and so on.

Summary

Joomla! is one of the best open source Content Management System. It is widely used for different types of websites. On the other hand, after HTML, CSS, and JavaScript, another widely used tool for web designers is Adobe Flash (previously known as Macromedia Flash). Although website design practices have been much improved for designing visually rich, interactive, and entertaining websites, Flash is still the best choice. This book shows you how to use Flash with Joomla! so that the power of these two combined can make your site an exceptional experience.

In this chapter we have briefly discussed why one should go for Joomla! and Flash together and what tools are required to do so. We have assumed that the readers of this book already have experience in Joomla! and Flash development. Therefore, we have just introduced some extra tools that will be useful for developing our Flash and Joomla!-based site. With this little introduction, in the next chapter, we move to building our site by adding Flash to the content of a Joomla! site.

2
Enhance Your Joomla! Content with Flash

Once you have set up Joomla!, configured it for its basic operation, and added some content, you can proceed to enhance the content by adding some extra flavor to it using Flash. We are assuming that by this time your Joomla! site is ready and you have added enough content, have placed the modules where needed, and applied a suitable template to it. With these assumptions, in this chapter, we will learn to:

- Add slideshows in Joomla! content with Flash animation effects
- Embed Shockwave animations in the content
- Display Flash objects on our site
- Display Flash movies in a separate module
- Embed Flash movies inside Joomla! content

For the purpose of this chapter, apart from downloading, installing, and configuring Joomla! extensions, you will not need to create any code or develop any module.

Have a look at the site!

Let us have a look at our present site. It is a simple web site made with Joomla! 1.5. A simple, freely available template — JW Clean Pro from `JoomlaWeb.com` — has been applied to the site. Some content has been added and the modules are placed at different positions in the template. The menus are still in their original format, but we will be changing the menus and logos and other elements in other chapters.

The site currently looks like the following screenshot:

As you can see, the default content of the site has not changed much, except for adding some new articles and rearranging the modules in the new template's module positions. Throughout this chapter we will add some more articles to demonstrate the skills we are learning.

Adding slideshows

Slideshows are common to many web sites. The basic principle of image slideshows is that images of a certain type and size are kept in a folder in the web directory. The underlying code in the web application reads the images and displays them one after another with some animation effects. The animation effects, the duration of displaying each image, and other settings can be controlled through some variables.

In Joomla!, there is one module called **Random Images**, mod_random_images. It reads the images of specified types from a specified directory and displays one image at a time. It's very simple! In order to use this module point to **Extensions | Module Manager** while logged in as an administrator to Joomla!. In the **Module Manager** screen, click on the module named **Random Image**. That opens the **Module: [Edit]** screen for the mod_random_image module as shown in the following screenshot:

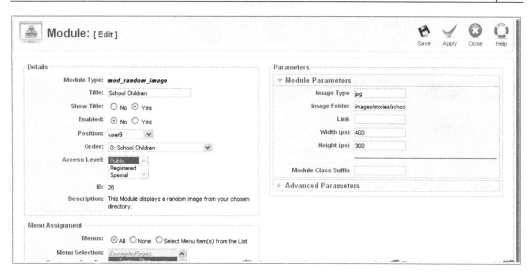

From the **Details** section, you can give a title to this module, select whether to show this title, enable or disable the module, select the position where to display this module, select the order, and optionally, select on what part of the site this module should be displayed. The main settings specific to this module are in the **Parameters** section.

In the **Parameters** section, first select the image types to be displayed. By default, the extension for JPEG image files **jpg** is provided here. You can add other image file extensions such as .png, .gif, and so on. You can specify only one file extension here, not multiple.

In the **Image Folder** field, type the path of the directory from which the images will be displayed. This path should be relative to the site path, for example, our path is images/stories/schoolchildren. If you want to link the images to be shown to a site or some pages in your site, then provide the link URL in the **Link** field. Then, specify the **Width** and **Height** of the image in pixels (**px**). Provide this size based on the module position; otherwise the image will be out of place.

Once all of this information is given, click on the **Save** or the **Apply** button on the toolbar. Now browse through your site, and you will find something similar to the following screenshot:

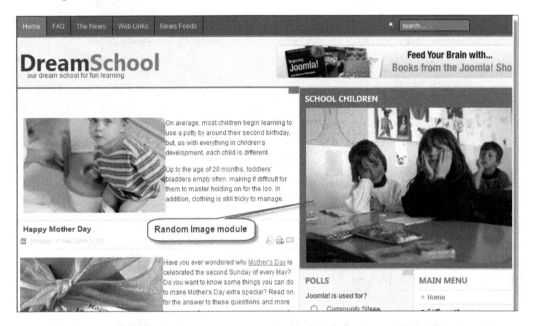

Now you can see our newly added **School Children** module that displays one .jpg image at a time from the specified images/stories/schoolchildren directory. The image displayed will not change until you refresh the page. In fact, it is a simple way to display any randomly-chosen image (without adding any animation or sliding effect). Technically speaking, this is called an image rotator, rather than an image slideshow. But most of you probably want more than this. That is possible with other slideshow modules. However, we will be looking in to one slideshow module that can create Flash animation effects for such slideshows.

Using RokSlideShow

RokSlideShow is one of the popular slideshow modules freely available. You can check its reviews and get the download link at http://extensions.joomla.org/ extensions/photos-&-images/images-slideshow/2078/details. Download the latest version (at the time of writing it was version 3.0.3), and install it from **Extensions | Install/Uninstall** screen in the Joomla! administration panel. Once downloaded and installed, you will find the module in the **Extensions | Module Manager** screen. Click on the module named **RokSlide Show** (in the type drop-down list it is mod_rokslideshow). This opens the **Module: [Edit]** screen for the mod_rokslideshow module.

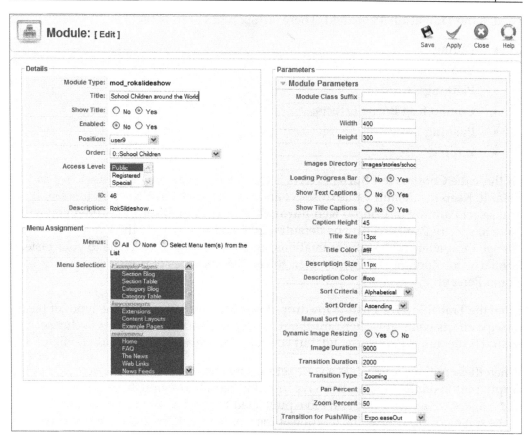

Like the other modules, the main configuration for this module is in the **Parameters** section too. After setting the options in the **Details** section, change the settings in the **Parameters** section. First you may like to set the **Width** and **Height** of the images, both in pixels, to be displayed on screen. Then comes the important part of specifying the image directory. As in the previous module, this should be a path relative to the Joomla! root. We will use the same image folder, `images/stories/schoolchildren`.

For the next three fields, **Loading Progress Bar**, **Show Text Captions**, and **Show Title Captions**, select **Yes**. Later on we will see how to display captions. Other fields below these are also related to caption and description texts. The default values for these fields will be fine for most cases. Select **Yes** for the **Dynamic Image Resizing** field. This will make your images of the same size and the slideshow will look consistent. In the **Image Duration** field, specify, in milliseconds, the duration for which an image should be displayed. In the **Transition Duration** field, specify how long the transition from one image to another should take.

Next is the **Transition Type** field. There are six types of transition:

- **Fading**
- **Zooming**
- **Panning**
- **Combo Ken Burns Effects**
- **Pushing**
- **Wiping**

Of these the **Combo Ken Burns Effects** is the most eye catching and is also set as default. Keep the default value or select another type of transition from this list. If you select **Panning** or **Combo Ken Burns Effects** as **Transition Type**, then you will have to specify **Pan Percent**. The default is 50% and that will do the work. You may change this value and test the animations, and later readjust the value to your taste. Similarly, for **Zooming** or **Combo Ken Burns Effects** types of transition, specify **Zoom Percent**.

From the **Transition for Push/Wipe** drop-down list, you can specify the types of push or wipe effects you want. There are about 30 MooTools transition effects to choose from. The default is **Expo.easeOut,** but you may choose another effect as you like.

When these options are set, save your settings by clicking on the **Save** or **Apply** button on the toolbar. We have unpublished the previously published `mod_random_image` module and have published the `mod_rokslideshow` module in the same position. Now the module at the frontend will look like the one shown in the following screenshot:

This time the module will display the pictures in the specified directory one-by-one, with the transition effect we have specified. What is missing here is that we don't see the captions or the titles of the images. We can add that too! The following section describes how to use captions and descriptions for this image slideshow.

Showing captions and descriptions for images

As you have seen, the RokSlideShow module can show the slideshow, taking all the images (.jpg, .png, and .gif) from a specified directory. We can also enable this module to display a caption and a description for each image. For this we need to create one .txt file with the same name as the image. For example, if the name of an image is computers.jpg, then there will be a computers.txt file. This file will contain the following three lines:

```
Children with computers
http://www.laptop.org
Children with computers at school. Luxury or necessity?
```

The first line is the caption of the image. Keep it short and succinct. The second line contains the URL where the users will be redirected on clicking that image. The third line is a little description of the image. This text may not be displayed fully if you do not adjust **Caption Height** in the module's **Parameters** section. If you do not want to link the image to any page or site, then type # at the start of the second line. For every image file you have to create one .txt file, as shown at the start of this section. The images/stories/schoolchildren directory will therefore appear as shown in the following screenshot:

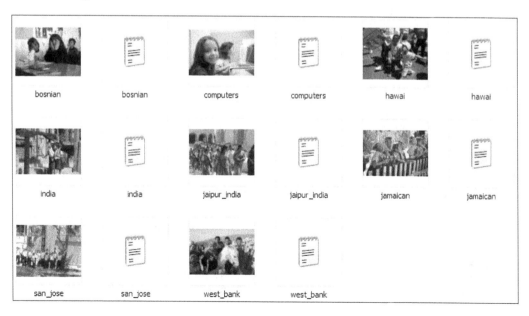

Now we can look into our site. Go to your site's frontend and refresh the front page. The module will now be displayed with the respective caption and description. The above mentioned image, `computers.jpg`, will display its corresponding caption and description from the `computers.txt` file. This is shown in the following screenshot:

When writing the `.txt` file for captions and descriptions, in the second line, specify the full URL, such as `http://www.laptop.org`, do not type only `www.laptop.org`. Otherwise, clicking on the image will try to connect to `localhost`. Therefore, always specify the full URL including the protocol.

Adding the slideshow to Joomla! articles

Adding the image slideshow is very simple with RokSlideShow. However, you may be wondering how to include this image slideshow into your articles. This can be done using another plugin for Joomla!, Modules Anywhere. Once it is installed, you can include any module in Joomla! articles and even inside other modules. You can get the details about this plugin and get a download link at `http://www.nonumber.nl/modulesanywhere`. Using this plugin, adding the RokSlideshow module will also be possible. For that, first you need to configure `mod_rokslideshow` with your desired set of images. The best way is to create a new module based on `mod_rokslideshow` and then including that into your article. The following sections show you how to do this.

After downloading and installing the Modules Anywhere plugin, go to **Extensions | Plugin Manager**. In the **Plugin Manager** screen, click on the name of the plugin, **System – Modules Anywhere**. That opens the **Plugin: [Edit]** screen. From the **Details** section, enable this plugin by clicking **Yes** in the **Enabled** field. Configure the plugin from the **Parameters** section, which looks like the following screenshot:

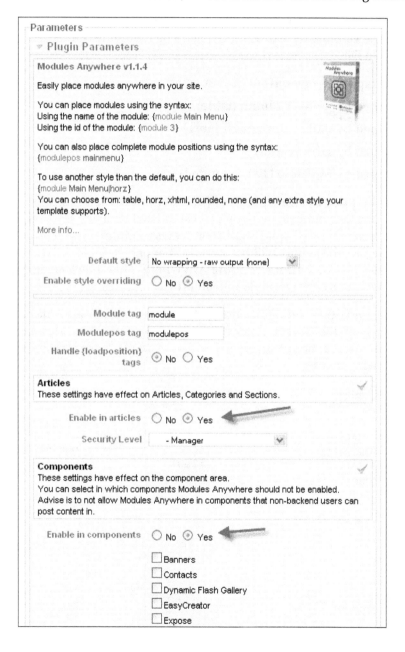

As you can see, the **Parameters** section explains how to use this plugin. It has two forms of syntax: `{module Module Name or id}` and `{modulepos module position name}`. For example, if we want to show the **Latest News** module in an article, we can simply type `{module Latest News}` in that article. It will include the contents displayed in the **Latest News** module.

The plugin can display the output in five formats, and you can select your preferred format from the **Default style** drop-down list. The following options are available in this drop-down list:

- **No Wrapping - raw output (none)**
- **Wrapped by table - Column (table)**
- **Wrapped by table - Horizontal (horz)**
- **Wrapped by Divs (xhtml)**
- **Wrapped by Multiple Divs (rounded)**

Let us select **Wrapped by Multiple Divs (rounded)** from the drop-down list. The words in the brackets indicate that you can use this while using the plugin syntax. For example, you want to display the **Latest News** module's output as a vertical column. Therefore, the syntax will be `{module Latest News|table}`. You can also activate another plugin, **Editor – Module Anywhere**. This shows an editor button with which you can insert a module into an article.

In the security and other settings sections, choose the appropriate options and click on the **Save** icon on the toolbar. After enabling the **System - Modules Anywhere** plugin, we can insert a module in an article. For example, if we publish an article with the following text:

```
School children around the world have different dresses, colors and
school buildings, but they have one common goal: to learn the lessons
needed to be a good human being. Look at the pictures taken from the
different parts of the world: they have different looks, different
environment, some are more privileged than others, but we see all are
enjoying the life - with great smiles!
{module School Children around the World!}
```

As the above article will include the `School Children around the World!` module, it will look like the following screenshot:

Using this plugin you can always include some module in the content articles. If you have installed several Flash modules and want to display some of them in an article, this plugin can help you.

Showing Flash in modules

There are several modules available that can be used to display Flash objects on a Joomla! site through a module. When displayed as a module, the Flash object can be shown in any module position. The following section describes the use of some of the popular modules for displaying Flash objects on a Joomla! site.

The Flash Module

The Flash Module is a module for adding Flash objects to your website. This is shown as a module and is good for showing a Flash menu, a Flash header, and other animations in module positions. You can download the Joomla! 1.5 native version of this module from `http://joomlacode.org/gf/project/flashmod/frs/`. The current version for Joomla! 1.5 is version 3.0.2.

Once downloaded, install it from the **Extensions | Install/Uninstall** screen. Then go to **Extensions | Module Manager**, and click on **The Flash Module**. That opens the **Module: [Edit]** screen for **The Flash Module**. As usual, from the left side of the screen, you can provide a title for the module, enable or disable the module, select the position where it will be displayed, select an order of display, access level, and specify the menus from where this will be visible.

The main settings for this module are available in the **Parameters** section of the **Module:[Edit]** screen, as shown in the following screenshot:

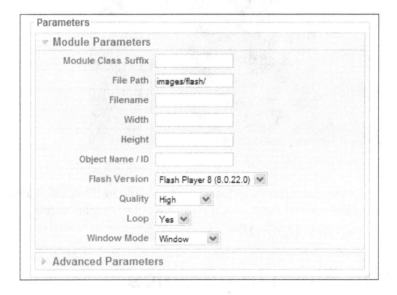

In the **Module Parameters** section you need to define the following parameters for this module:

- **File Path**: Specify the path of the folder where the flash files are stored on your web server. The default path is `images/flash`, which will be fine for if you keep your SWF files in the `flash` sub-directory under the `images` directory in Joomla's web root.

- **Filename**: This is the filename of the SWF file that is to be displayed in the module.

- **Width**: Specify the width of the module in pixels.

- **Height**: Specify the height of the module in pixels.

- **Object Name / ID**: Provide a name for the object or type an ID for the object.

- **Flash Version**: Select the version of Flash player required to play the embedded Flash object. The version of the Flash player will be downloaded to the user's computer if needed.

- **Quality**: Select the quality of the Flash playback. The available options in this drop-down list are **Best, High, Medium, Low, Auto High**, and **Auto Low**. This setting will be used in the Flash player.

- **Loop**: To get the looping effect in the Flash playback, select **Yes** in this drop-down list.

- **Window Mode**: For transparency, layering, and positioning of the Flash movie in the browser, select the **Window Mode** property. There are three options available in this drop-down list: **Window, Opaque**, and **Transparent**.

Below the **Parameters** section, you find the **Advanced Parameters** section. This is as shown in the following screenshot:

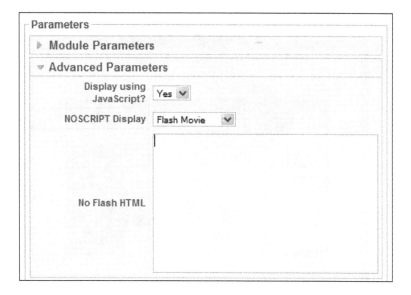

You can configure the following parameters from the **Advanced Parameters** section:

- **Display using JavaScript?**: A Flash animation or any other object can be embedded into your site using JavaScript. Use of JavaScript can overcome errors that are usually displayed by Internet Explorer. Therefore, it is better to select **Yes** from this drop-down list.

- **NOSCRIPT Display**: Some browsers may not detect the JavaScript used for embedding Flash objects. In that case you may show the embedded Flash object using a direct embedding tag or display some HTML tag specified in the **No Flash HTML** box. Select **Flash Movie** to display the Flash object, or select **No-Flash HTML** to display the text specified in the **No Flash HTML** field.

- **No Flash HTML**: Type the text that should be displayed as the **No Flash HTML** message. If the browser does not detect JavaScript and **NOSCRIPT Display** is set to **No-Flash HTML**, then the text specified in this field will be displayed to the visitors.

When configured with the appropriate values in these fields and once the module is enabled, the module looks as shown in the following screenshot:

Note that by using Flash Module, you can publish one SWF object at a time, not many with random selection and display. However, other modules such as the one discussed in the next section can take a random Flash object from the directory and display that to the visitors.

Joomla! Random Flash Module

The Flash Module discussed in the previous section displays a Flash object from the specified folder. You can specify the directory for Flash files. However, you cannot select a random SWF file from that directory and display that animation. Joomla! Random Flash Module does the same thing like Flash Module, but it also adds the functionality of randomly choosing an SWF file from the specified directory.

You can get the module from `http://www.dart-creations.com/Joomla/Joomla-Modules/Joomla-Random-Flash-Module.html`. After downloading and installing it from the **Extensions | Install/Uninstall** screen, go to **Extensions | Module Manager** and click on **Joomla! 1.5 Random Flash Module**. That brings up the **Module: [Edit]** screen from where you can provide a title for this module, enable it, and set the position for displaying this module. The module-specific settings are in the **Parameters** section, shown in the following screenshot, and are similar to the settings for Flash Module discussed in the previous section.

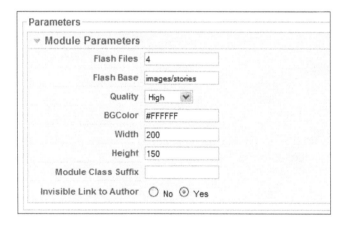

As we see, here too we need to specify the name of the folder that will contain the Flash objects. Then specify the background color, the height, and the width. The **Flash Files** field indicates the number of files present in that directory. If there are five files in the Flash base directory (`images/stories` or `images/flash`), then specify **5** in the **Flash Files** field. For viewing the Flash files in this module, you need to put the files in this directory and rename them with names like `1.swf`, `2.swf`, `3.swf`, and so on. This renaming is important as other names will not work with this module. When configured in this way and when the module is published, it will display a randomly selected Flash file from that directory. The Flash file will change every time the page is refreshed.

Adding Flash movies using Simple Video Flash Player

There are some modules available in the Joomla! Extensions Directory that can be used for displaying Flash movies on your site. Some of them are very nice, and Simple Video Flash Player is one such module. You can download it from `http://www.joomlaos.de/Joomla_CMS_Downloads/Joomla_Module/ Simple_Video_Flash_Player.html`.

This module can play a single video or multiple videos from the playlist. It can also play YouTube videos and supports the following file formats:

- FLV7 (video)
- FLV8 (video)
- H.264 (video)
- Youtube (video)
- MP3 (audio)
- AAC (audio)
- JPG (images)
- GIF (images)
- PNG (images)

As we have mentioned already, it can play videos from a playlist. It supports multiple types of video playlists such as:

- ASX
- ATOM
- RSS + iTunes
- RSS + Media
- SMIL
- XSPFI

 If you are not familiar with these formats, then please search on the web and find the specifications. We will be using the ATOM playlist format for our example here. For further details of the file formats supported and links to their specifications, visit `http://www.time2online.de/joomla-extensions`.

Showing Flash movie in a module

Once you have downloaded and installed the Simple Video Flash Player module, go to **Extensions | Module Manager** and click on **Simple Video Flash Player Module**. That opens the **Module:[Edit]** screen for Simple Video Flash Player Module. As usual, from the **Details** and the **Menu Assignment** section, set the common settings for modules—provide a name for this module and publish this module in your preferred module position. The module-specific settings are in the **Parameters** section.

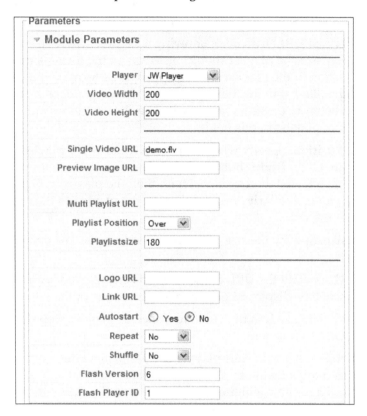

You need to configure the following options for this module:

- **Player**: Select the player you want to use. There are three types of players available—**JW Player**, **Mini Player**, and **Youtube Player**. Each of these players have a different look. The default is **JW Player**. If you wish to use some other player such as **Youtube Player**, then select it from this drop-down list.

- **Video Width** and **Video Height**: Specify the width and height of the Flash video player. It does not have to be the same size as the video you want to play.

- **Single Video URL**: When trying to play a single video, you can add the URL of that video to this field. For example, to show a video from YouTube, add the URL of that video such as `http://www.youtube.com/watch?v=iS_sPFh9B30`. If you have uploaded the video to your web server, then specify the URL of that file.

- **Preview Image URL**: Specify the URL of the preview image for the video. It is better to provide a preview image than showing a blank screen on the video. This preview image will be displayed until the video starts playing. The image can be in `.jpg`, `.gif`, or `.png` format.

- **Multi Playlist URL**: Instead of showing a single video, you can show videos from a playlist. The playlist should be in any of the formats mentioned in the earlier section. If the playlist is in an appropriate format, you can specify the URL of the playlist in this field. If you are showing videos from YouTube, then it is better to create a playlist with the chosen videos and specify the URL of that playlist in this field.

- **Playlist Position**: Specify where you wish to show the playlist. The available options are **Over**, **Right**, **Bottom**, and **None**. Select **None** if you do not wish to show the playlist. If you select **Over**, then the playlist will be displayed over the video. Similarly, you can display the playlist to the right or at the bottom of the video.

- **Playlistsize**: Specify the size of the playlist in pixels. The default size is **180** pixels.

- **Logo URL**: Specify the URL of the Logo to be displayed with the video. This logo will be displayed on the top-right corner of the video.

- **Link URL**: You can link the video to a specific page or web site. Just enter the link URL to this field.

- **Autostart**: Select **Yes** to start playing the video just after loading the page. Often you may not want to play the video automatically. In such a case, select **No**. The visitor will then have to click on the start button on the video player to start playing the video.

- **Repeat**: The video can be repeated automatically. If you want to repeat all the videos — both a single video and videos from playlist — then select **Always** from this drop-down list. Selecting **List** will repeat only the videos played from the playlist. Select **None** to not repeat the playing of any video.

- **Shuffle**: When playing videos from the playlist, their order of playing can be shuffled. Select **Shuffle** from this drop-down list to enable the shuffling feature.

- **Flash Version**: Specify the Flash version needed to play the video. The default is 6, which is fine for most videos.
- **Flash Player ID**: Specify the Flash Player ID. This is to identify the Flash player and will be beneficial for scripting.

Let us first try showing a single video on our site. We will play a video from YouTube. Browse through YouTube and find a video that you want to show on your web site. In our case, the URL of this video is `http://www.youtube.com/watch?v=iS_sPFh9B30`. If you have tried this URL by this time, you'll find that it's a nursery rhyme. Quite suitable for our DreamSchool site! To embed this, we type this URL in the **Single Video URL** field. We then specify the **Width** and **Height** as **400** and **350** pixels respectively. Once the module is published we see the YouTube video as shown in the following screenshot:

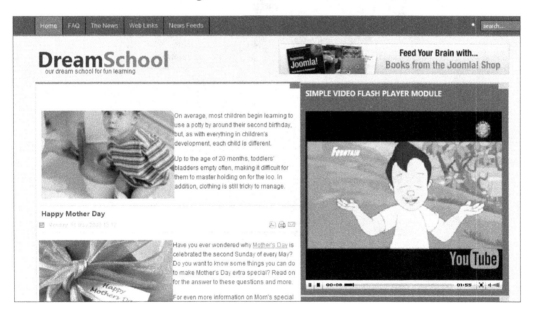

Now we will be looking at how to show a bunch of videos by building a video playlist. As we have already seen how to use YouTube videos on our site, let us try another video sharing site—Metacafe (www.metacafe.com). Let us go to Metacafe and search with the keywords 'Nursery Rhymes'. We will get a big list of videos with these two keywords. On the toolbar we see the RSS icon. We simply copy the link URL for this RSS icon and paste it in the **Multi Playlist URL** field. We get a URL similar to http://www.metacafe.com/tags/nursery_rhymes/rss.xml. This file is in the RSS + Media format. With this URL pasted, let us publish the module. We will see the **Simple Video Flash Player** module, as shown in the following screenshot:

As you can see, the playlist is shown on the right side of the player. You can scroll down and click on any video icon to play it. Now, we want to display the playlist at the bottom of the main video player screen so that we can read the names of the videos in the playlist. For doing so, select **Bottom** in the **Playlist Position** field and adjust the value in the **Playlistsize** field. With these changes, the module will look like the following screenshot:

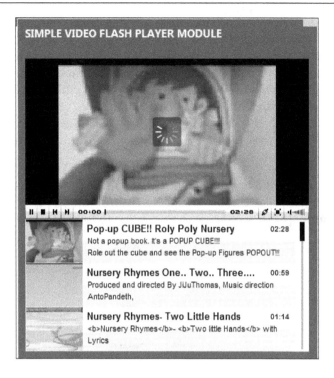

You can experiment further with the size and position of the playlist.

 You can also create your own RSS + Media file. For a good tutorial on how to do so, visit http://developer.truveo.com/ DirectorDocumentation.php. For a reference on using RSS + Media XML files, please go to http://search.yahoo.com/mrss/.

Showing a Flash movie in content

So far we have seen how to display Flash videos in modules. The Simple Flash Video Player can show different types of Flash videos (and also audio) in module positions. What about showing these types of videos in the articles? Sometimes it is necessary to show article related videos. For example, on our DreamSchool website, we are trying to teach how to fix a bicycle tyre puncture. We may describe the procedures step by step, and also, we may add a video to demonstrate how to do that. In such a case, embedding the Flash video within the article will be convenient.

For embedding videos from online streaming services, from your own server, or a remote server into your articles, you can use a single plugin, AllVideos, available from `http://www.joomlaworks.gr/`. It can embed almost all types of videos, including more than 30 video services, from your own server or a remote server. Its syntax is also very easy and descriptive. For example, if we want to embed a single video from YouTube, we can just include it with a code like `{youtube}youtube_video_id {/youtube}`. You can embed an FLV video that resides in the default folder with a code like `{flv}my_flv_video{/flv}`. Similarly, an MP3 audio file can be embedded with the code `{mp3}my_mp3_filename{/mp3}`.

Once you have downloaded and installed the AllVideos plugin, go to **Extensions | Plugin Manager**, and click on the **AllVideos** (from **JoomlaWorks**) plugin. That brings up the **Plugin: [Edit]** screen, as shown in the following screenshot:

```
Parameters
   ▽ Plugin Parameters

   Choose AllVideos layout     Default ▾

   Compress player scripts     ○ No  ⦿ Yes
              using PHP

                              =========== VIDEO PARAMETERS ===========

        Local Video Folder     images/stories/videos

   Default width (in px) for   400
                  videos

   Default height (in px) for  300
                  videos

                              =========== AUDIO PARAMETERS ===========

        Local Audio Folder     images/stories/audio

   Default width (in px) for   300
              audio player

   Default height (in px) for  20
              audio player

                              =========== GLOBAL PARAMETERS ===========

              Autoplay         ⦿ No  ○ Yes

        Player transparency    ○ No  ⦿ Yes

   Player background color     #ffffff

                              =========== FLV PLAYBACK ===========

   Player controlbar location  ⦿ Bottom  ○ Over

              Debug Mode        ⦿ Disabled  ○ Enabled
```

As with other plugins, you can enable the AllVideos plugin from the **Details** section by selecting **Yes** in the **Enabled** field. Then, configure its parameters from the **Parameters** section. The first parameter you need to configure is **AllVideos layout**. You can select either **Default** or **Sleek** from this drop-down list. If you want to compress the JavaScript to enhance performance, select **Yes** in the **Compress players scripts using PHP** field. If you are storing the videos on your server, specify the path to the server in the **Local Video Folder** field. By default, this is set to `images/stories/videos`; you can keep it like this to avoid any permission-related problems. Then specify the width and height for the videos in pixels. The default is 400 and 300 pixels respectively.

As you can embed audio files too, you need to specify the web server's path in the **Local Audio Folder** field. The default value for this field is `images/stories/audio`, which should be fine for most of the cases. Like videos, you can also set the width and height of the audio player.

Select **Yes** for the **Autoplay** field to enable automatic playback of the video or the audio file embedded on the webpage. Moreover, you can set the transparency of the player from the **Player transparency** field. Specify the player's background color if you don't like the default color. At the end, you can specify the **Player controlbar location**. This can be set to either **Bottom** or **Over**.

Once the plugin is configured and enabled, we can embed the video and audio files within the Joomla! content. The generic syntax for embedding video or audio using this plugin is as follows:

```
{format/provider}filename{/format/provider}
```

You can either use the format name or the provider's name in the starting and closing tag. Then specify the name of the file to be embedded. For example, consider that we want to add a video from YouTube. We need to know the filename. In fact, we need the video code shown after the word `watch` in the URL. Hence, the syntax for embedding the YouTube video will be:

```
{youtube}filename{/youtube}
```

You can also use file format as tags. For example, if you want to add an FLV file, then the code for it will be as shown here:

```
{flv}filename{/flv}
```

When we embed the videos or audios without specifying any parameters, they are displayed with the default parameters set for the plugin. However, you can set the parameters with the embedding code too. The syntax for adding parameters is as follows:

```
{format/provider}filename|width|height|autoplay{/format/provider}
```

As you see, you can specify the `width`, `height`, and `autoplay` options for a video or an audio file. For example, while adding a YouTube video we can specify the parameters as follows:

```
{youtube}SGwQxTfApCg|600|450|true{/youtube}
```

Adding this line of code in an article will display the video, as shown in this screenshot:

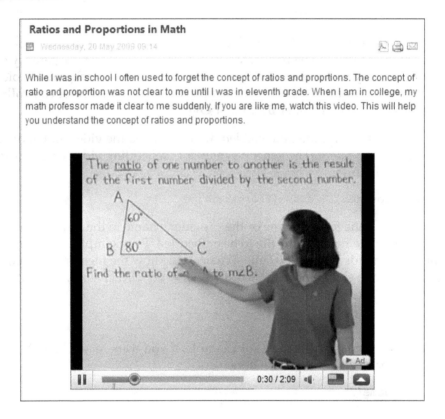

Ratios and Proportions in Math

Wednesday, 20 May 2009 09:14

While I was in school I often used to forget the concept of ratios and proprtions. The concept of ratio and proportion was not clear to me until I was in eleventh grade. When I am in college, my math professor made it clear to me suddenly. If you are like me, watch this video. This will help you understand the concept of ratios and proportions.

If we save the video file as `math_ratio.flv` in the `images/stories/videos` folder, then we can simply embed the video using `{flv}math_ratio{/flv}`. This will display the same video too. We may also use any other online video sharing service. For example, to embed a video from Dailymotion (`http://www.dailymotion.com/`), we can use the following code:

```
{dailymotion}x92fmm_national-childrens-day-2009_news{/dailymotion}
```

This will show the video as shown in the following screenshot:

As we have seen so far, embedding any video within the Joomla! content is very easy using the AllVideos plugin. The plugin can be obtained for free and can be used on your site. The configuration for the plugin is simple and straightforward.

For more information on the AllVideos plugin and its usage, go to `http://www.joomlaworks.gr/content/view/16/42/`.

Summary

In this chapter we have looked into some of the details of adding Flash animations and videos into our Joomla!-based site. First, we learned to add any Flash animation to our web site and display that in different module positions. Next, we included the animations in Joomla! content such as articles. Towards the end, we learned how to add Flash videos on a Joomla! site as a module as well as in the content. We have learned about several Joomla! extensions that can be used for enhancing the Joomla! content with Flash animations and videos.

With this acquired skill, we will now be trying to enhance our site further by redesigning the menus using Flash. In the next chapter we will learn about creating attractive menus using Flash.

3
Creating Attractive Menus with Flash

So far we have used the traditional Joomla! look and feel. By this time, we have also learned how to use Flash objects with Joomla! content. In the previous chapter we saw how to embed slideshows with Flash effects, display Flash animations in Joomla! modules and articles, and display Flash videos in content. Now we will see how to change the look and feel of our website. In this chapter we will be looking into changing the menus of a Joomla!-based site. On the completion of this chapter you will be able to:

- Understand the difference between Joomla! built-in menus and Flash-based menus
- Make menus more attractive using Flash
- Use different extensions for customizing menus as per your needs

This chapter assumes that you have basic knowledge of the Joomla! menu system and that you can configure Joomla! menus.

The existing Joomla! menu system

Joomla! has an excellent menu system, which can be considered as one of the best menu management systems in the CMS arena. You can build your own menus and display these in different positions as modules. You can see the built-in menus from **Menus | Menu Manager**. This displays the **Menu Manager** screen, as shown in the following screenshot:

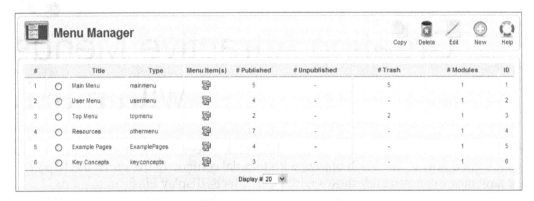

To create a new menu, click on the **New** button on the toolbar, provide a name for the menu, and save it. For adding/editing items in a menu, click on the icon in the **Menu Item(s)** column. This will display the **Menu Item Manager** screen for that menu as shown in the following screenshot:

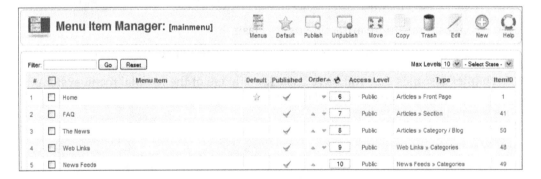

For creating a new menu item click on the **New** button and follow the wizard. It asks you to select a menu type, specify the link and title, and finally save it.

The built-in menu system in Joomla! is quite good and applicable for almost all types of websites. However, for making it an eye-candy, website designers prefer to use some other modules or components with it. Flash developers may also like to add Flash menus with animation. In that case, Flash menus can be used with some third-party extensions.

Making menus attractive using Flash

We have already seen that Joomla! has a strong menu-management system through which we can create multiple menus and menu items. These menus can be displayed using modules. Several third-party Joomla! extensions are available to make cosmetic changes in these menus, particularly to display menus with some animation effects. There are also some extensions for adding Flash menus into a Joomla! website. However, in this chapter, we will be limiting our discussions to the freely available Flash menu extension and the demo version of Super Web Flash module.

Flash Floating Menu

The only free extension in the Joomla! Extensions Directory for adding Flash menus in Joomla! sites is Flash Floating Menu. With this extension you can add floating Flash menus to your Joomla! site. In fact, you don't need to create any Flash menu, instead you just have to specify the icons, links, and tips for those links. The module will create the animated Flash menu. When you move your cursor over any icon, you will see a tip just like those in Flash menus. This extension is comprised of two extensions:

- one component—`com_flashmenu`
- one module—`mod_flashmenu`

You can download this extension for free from `http://www.webmaster-tips.net/Download/View-details/1-Joomla-Modules/174-Joomla-1.5-Module-Flash-Menu.html` after registering on the site.

Both the component and module come in a single ZIP file. Unzip the downloaded `J15_Module_FlashMenu_extract_first.zip` file. You should then see two ZIP files: `com_flashmenu.zip` and `mod_flashmenu.zip`. You need to install both, the component and the module, from the **Extensions | Install/Uninstall** screen. Once the two files have been installed, you need to configure the component and then configure and publish the module. Instructions for doing so are provided in the `configuration.txt` file bundled with the package.

Using the component

Using Flash Floating Menu is simple; you assign menu icons, links, and corresponding tips for links. This assignment can be done using the component in this package. To configure the menu icons and links, go to **Components | Flash Menu | Configure**. This shows the **Flash Menu** screen, as shown in the following screenshot:

As you can see, the toolbar has icons for creating new icons, uploading icons, publishing, unpublishing, and configuring icons. By default, you see some of the icons configured. You can keep those icons or delete them completely. It is advisable to upload all the icons first. The icons must be in the .png, .jpg, or .gif formats. Icon sizes should be 32 x 32, 64 x 64, 128 x 128, and 256 x 256 pixels.

Once you have designed and saved the icons in an appropriate format, you can upload them to your Joomla! site for use with the Flash Floating menu. For uploading an icon, click on the **Upload Icon** button on the toolbar. This shows the upload screen for the icon, shown in the this screenshot:

Click on the **Browse…** button and select the icon you want to upload. Click on the **Upload Icon** button to upload the icon image to your web server. Now you can use this icon to create a link.

To create a menu link click on the **New Icon** button on the toolbar. This brings up the **Edit icon menu** screen, as shown in the following screenshot:

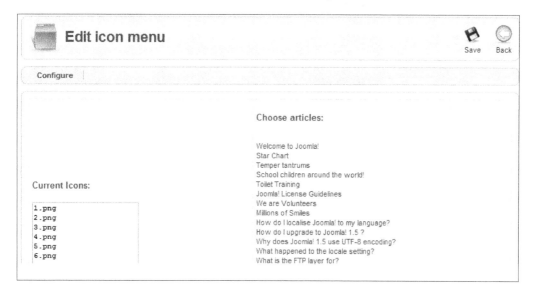

In the **Current Icons** section you will see a list of the existing icons defined. Below this list there is a form to define a new icon, as shown in the next screenshot. On the right, you will see the list of Joomla! articles from which you can select one to link with an icon.

Image:	
	* flash menu icon name
Tooltip:	
	* tooltip under icon (on mouse over)
Action:	http://
	* link to: enter URL or SELECT Article ITEM

In the **Image** field, type the name of the icon image file that you have uploaded already, for example, download.png. You don't need to specify the directory path, but never forget to specify the file extension. In the **Tooltip** field, type the tooltip to be shown when the cursor passes over this icon. On mouse over, this text will be displayed below the icon. Then comes the important part of linking the icon to an article or a section of your site. In the **Action** field, specify the URL of the section of your site that you wish to link to. If you want to link to a specific article, then you can do that by typing the URL of that article or by clicking on the title of an article from the list of articles displayed on the right of this screen. Once all these three fields — **Image**, **Tooltip**, and **Action** — have been configured, you can publish the icon by selecting **Yes** from the **Published** drop-down list. Finally you click on the **Save** icon on the toolbar.

There are some global configurations for the icons and their sizes. You can configure these by clicking on the **Config** icon on the toolbar in the **Flash menu** screen. This shows the **Edit icon menu** screen, as shown in the following screenshot:

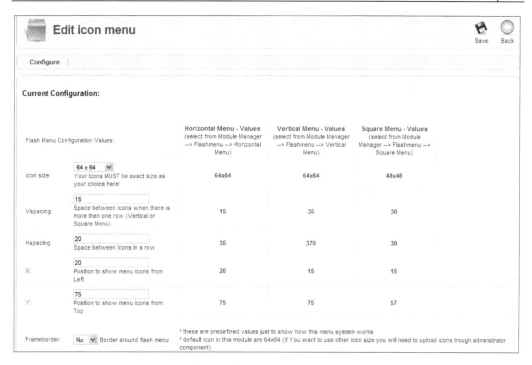

The screen displays the current configuration. From the **Icon size** drop-down list, you can select an icon size. The default is **64 x 64** pixels. However you can select **32 x 32**, **48 x 48**, **64 x 64**, **128 x 128**, or **256 x 256**. The uploaded icon images have to be of the same size selected from this list. You need to resize the images manually before uploading them for the Flash menu using the icon uploader that we have seen earlier.

Flash menu can display three types of menus: Horizontal menu, Vertical menu, and Square menu. The **Edit icon menu** screen also shows the settings for these three types of menus. You can configure how the menus will be displayed—horizontal, vertical, or square—while configuring the Flash menu module, mod_flashmenu. If the menu icons are displayed in more than one row, then you need to specify the vertical spacing in the **Vspacing** field. The default value for vertical spacing is **15** pixels. Similarly, you can specify the horizontal spacing between icons too. Specify the horizontal spacing in the **Hspacing** field. The default value for horizontal spacing is **20** pixels, which you can change based on the size of the icons you are using.

From the **X** and **Y** fields, you can specify where to display the icons. In the **X** field, specify the position of the icon from the left of the screen, and in the **Y** field, specify the position of the icon from the top of the screen.

When published with the default settings and in horizontal alignment, the **Flash Menu Module** will look like the following screenshot:

There is an animated effect when the cursor moves over the icon. The tooltip for the icon is, generally, not visible, but it is visible when the mouse cursor moves over an icon. Clicking on the icon will take you to the linked URL.

You can display a border around the Flash menu by selecting **Yes** in the **Frameborder** drop-down list in the **Edit icon menu** screen. Once the frame border has been enabled, the Flash menu shown in the previous screenshot will look like the one shown in following the screenshot:

Once you have configured the global settings for the Flash menu icons, you can save the settings by clicking on the **Save** icon on the toolbar. After configuring the global settings, we can proceed to configuring and publishing the Flash menu module (mod_flashmenu).

Using the module

If you have not installed the Flash menu module yet, then install it from the **Extensions | Install/Uninstall** screen. Once installed, you can configure it from **Extensions | Module Manager**. In the **Module Manager** screen, find the module named **Flashmenu** (mod_flashmenu), and click on it to edit it. This shows the **Module: [Edit]** screen for the Flash menu module, as shown in the following screenshot:

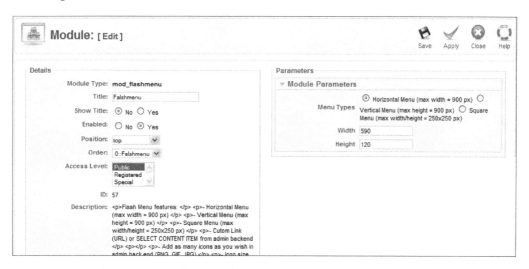

As with other modules, you specify the module's title in the **Title** field in the **Details** section. As you are showing this module as a menu, it is better to select **No** for the **Show Title** field. To publish this module select **Yes** in the **Enabled** field. In the **Position** drop-down list, select a module position where you want the module to be displayed. Be cautious about selecting the module position. If this is a horizontal module, then the position should have enough space (maximum 900 pixels) to show the menu items. The restriction of 900 pixels is set by this module, not by the template. For a vertical menu, it should have a similar amount of space to display the items. Generally, horizontal menus are displayed at the top or bottom positions, while the vertical or square menus can be displayed in the left or right positions.

Next, select an appropriate order of the modules to be displayed and the access level. If this module is used to show the main menu, set **Access Level** to **Public**. For private menus, set it to **Registered** or **Special**. In the **Description** field, you will see the configuration options for this module. It says that some settings can be modified from the Flash menu component. Like all other modules, you can set the visibility of this module too from its **Menu Assignment** section, as shown in the following screenshot:

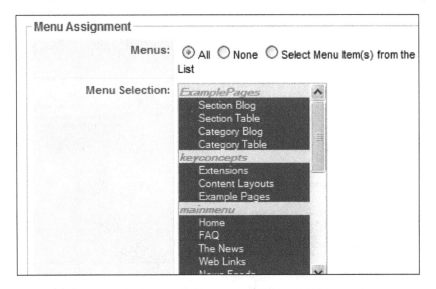

In this screen select **All** in the **Menus** field to display this menu in every section of your site. Alternatively, you can show this module in specific menu sections by clicking on **Select Menu Item(s) from the List** and selecting the menu items from the **Menu Selection** listbox.

Module-specific settings are in the **Parameters** section. Click on **Module Parameters**, and you will see a bunch of configuration options for this module, as shown in the following screenshot:

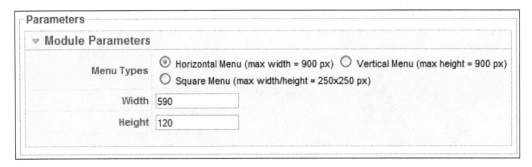

In the **Parameters** section you need to select the menu type. In the **Menu Types** field select a menu type. As discussed earlier, there are three types of menu – horizontal, vertical, and square. By default, **Horizontal Menu** is selected. Let us first try using the default menu (please note the maximum possible width for each type of menu). Then, in the **Width** and **Height** fields, specify the width and height of the module in pixels.

Once all these options are set, save the settings by clicking on the **Save** icon on the toolbar. Now preview the site, and you will find the Flash menu module in the specified position. The horizontal Flash menu will look like the one shown in the following screenshot:

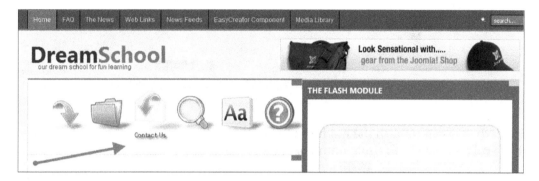

Now we want to see how to use this module as a vertical menu. For doing so, first select the module position as **Left**, as it will now be in a vertical position. Then simply change the settings in the **Parameters** section, as shown in the following screenshot:

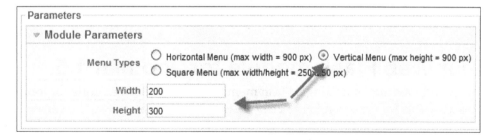

Once these settings have been saved and published, the module will be displayed on the module position 'left', as shown in the following screenshot:

Similarly, we can publish the module as a Square menu. In that case, you can specify the width and height to a maximum of 250 x 250 pixels.

By default, there are icons bundled with the module. However, you may like to use customized icons for different menu items. There are many tools with which you can create the icon images you want. But if you are not a graphic wizard or simply like to use ready made icon images, then you can download some free icon packs from the internet. A good site for finding icons is http://www.iconfinder.net.

Super Web Flash module for Joomla! 1.5

A really good module for adding a Flash menu is the Web Flash module for Joomla! 1.5. It is available for download at http://tinyurl.com/super-web-flash-mod. This is a commercial module. However, you can download a trial version for free. Visit the site and download the trial version of this module.

Once downloaded, you can install it from the **Extensions | Install/Uninstall** screen. Next, go to **Extensions | Module Manager** to configure and publish this module. From the **Module Manager** screen, click on the mod_web_flash module. This shows the **Module: [Edit]** screen for the Web Flash Joomla! 1.5 module, shown in the following screenshot:

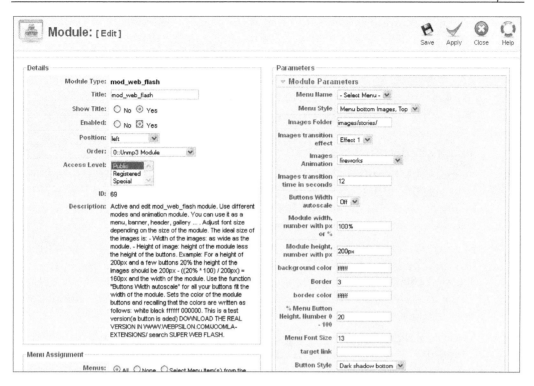

Like the other modules, you can configure this module too from the **Details** and the **Menu Assignment** sections. Enable the module and select a module position where you want the module to be displayed. Settings specific to this module are in the **Parameters** section. You have to configure the following options from the **Parameters** section:

- **Menu Name**: Select a menu name from the drop-down list. This drop-down list will display available menus built from the Joomla! menu manager. This module will display the menu based on the menu selected in this field.

- **Menu Style**: Select a style for the menu from this drop-down. For displaying the menu at the bottom and the image on top of the menu, select **Menu bottom Images, Top**. To display in reverse order, that is menu on the top and the image at the bottom, select **Menu top, Images bottom**. In order to just show the menu without an image, select **Only menu** from this drop-down list.

- **Images Folder:** Specify the path of the folder from which the images will be displayed in the Flash module. By default, this module displays images from the images/stories/ folder. For using other images, specify the directory path relative to the Joomla! installation directory.

- **Images transition effect**: Select a transition effect for the images from the drop-down list. You can select from three effects: **Effect1**, **Effect2**, and **Effect3**. Before choosing an effect from this list, you may first select and try the effect.

- **Images Animation**: Select an animation effect for the images from the drop-down list. There are about thirty animation effects to choose from.

- **Images transition time in seconds**: Specify the time for the transition of images. By default it is set to **12** seconds.

- **Buttons Width autoscale**: You can specify to autoscale the width of buttons based on the button text. Turning on the autoscaling of button widths will be logical as menu items may have different lengths of texts. To enable this, select **On** from the drop-down list.

- **Module width, number with px or** %: You can specify the module width in this field by either typing the width in the number of pixels or percentage. The percentage value will display the module width relative to the width of the module position. For example, a value of 20% in this field will make the module's width 20% of the width of the module position.

- **Module height, number with px:** Like the module width, you can specify a module's height in this field. You need to type the number of pixels for the height of the module.

- **background color**: Specify the background color of the module in this field. The value should be in hexadecimal format, for example, `ffffff`.

- **Border**: Specify the size of the border of the module. If you don't want a border, simply put 0 in this field.

- **border color**: Specify the border color in this field in hexadecimal format, for example, `cccccc`. This value will have no effect on the border if you set 0 in the **Border** field.

- % **Menu Button Height, Number 0-100**: Specify the height of the menu button as percentage of the height of the module. You can specify a value in the range of 0 to 100.

- **Menu Font Size**: Specify the font size for the menu buttons.

- **target link**: Select how the menu buttons should link. Selecting **_blank** in this field will open the linked resource in a new window. Specify **_self** to open the linked resource in the same window. Generally, remote resources are opened in a new window, whereas resources in the same site are opened in the same window.

- **Button Style**: You can select a button style from this drop-down list. The available options are: **Dark Shadow bottom**, **Dark shadow top**, and **None**.

- **Buttons background color, separated by intros**: You can specify a background color for each button. Type the background color in this textbox, each in a separate line. For example, if you have 5 menu items and want to show each button in a different color, specify 5 color in five lines in this textbox.

- **Buttons text color, separated by intros**: You can specify a text color for each button, in the same way as the background colors for the buttons. Specify the hexadecimal code for each color on a separate line.

- **Menu text font**: Specify the font that will be used to display the menu text. For example, Arial or Times New Roman.

- **Menu Button Width**: Specify the width of the menu buttons in pixels. By default the width of the menu button is **120** pixels. If menu texts exceed the width of the button, you may need to adjust this value accordingly.

- **Menu Button Separation**: Specify the space between buttons in pixels. By default, this space is set to **1** pixel. You may need to adjust this based on the number of buttons you want to show.

- **Button Text align**: You can specify the manner in which you want the button text to be aligned. Select an alignment from this drop-down list. The available options are **left**, **right**, and **center**.

- **Text in button if button is parent**: Specify the text to be shown when the button is a parent button, that is, it has other child menu items. The default text shown is **>>**, and you can change this from this field.

- **Images in the buttons?**: If you want to show images from the folder specified earlier in the **Images Folder** field to display as button, select **Yes** in this drop-down list. Otherwise, select **non** in this field.

- **Manual buttons Links separated by intros**: This is an important field for configuring the links or menu items manually. Type the link URLs in separate lines. For example, if you want to add five links, you need to type the URLs on five separate lines as shown in this screenshot:

Manual buttons Links separated by intros	http://www.packtpub.com http://www.joomla.org http://www.drupal.org http://www.wordpress.org http://www.zen-cart.com

In order for the links to function correctly you need to specify the complete URL. Using relative URLs will cause problems in locating the resource. Also note that when developing on your local server, the URLs may be different. Therefore, before uploading to the production server, you need to adjust these link URLs. If not, the links may malfunction.

- **Manual texts buttons separated by intros**: You can display specific texts for each menu button which were added manually in an earlier field. This text will be displayed on the buttons defined earlier. Type the text in this textbox separated by a line break. The texts will be displayed in the sequence in which you type it in this box. For the menu buttons we configured earlier, we may like to add some text as shown in the following screenshot:

Manual texts buttons separated by intros	Packt Publishing Joomla! Drupal WordPress Zen Cart

Once we have specified the texts as shown in this screenshot, we will see the menu buttons with the texts as shown in the following screenshot:

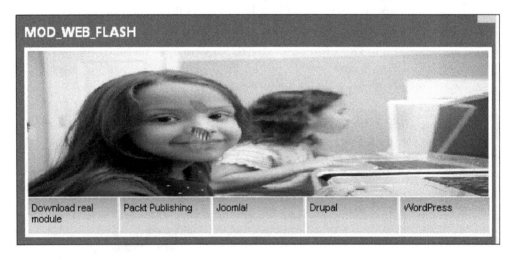

After setting all these options, click on the **Save** button on the toolbar to save the settings. As you have published the module in the top or the bottom module position, the module will be displayed in that position as a menu. One of the good things about this module is that we can use it as a banner too. In that case, we only assign background images, links, texts, texts, and so on without specifying the menu texts. Further, we set the background images along with the title and links. We will see its use as a banner in Chapter 6, *Flash Decorations: Flashy Templates, Headers, Banners, and Tickers*.

Some other extensions for creating Flash menus

So far we have seen the use of two modules for adding Flash menus in a Joomla!-based site. One of them is freely available, another is commercially licensed but you can download a free trial version. Most of the modules and components listed at http://extensions.joomla.org/extensions/core-enhancements/menu-systems/flash-menus are licensed commercially. The following are some such extensions that you can purchase and use with your Joomla! site:

- **JF Appliance Flash Menu**: JF Appliance is a Joomla! 1.5 native module for displaying Joomla! menus in a Flash format. You can select the Joomla! menu to be displayed in the Flash module. This is commercially licensed and can be purchased from http://joomla-flash.com/en/joomla-flash-menus/1-jf-appliance-joomla-flash-menu.html. A demo of the module is also available on this page.

- **Flash Blur Effect Menu**: This is another Joomla! 1.5 module for displaying the Flash menu with a blur effect. This commercially licensed module can be obtained from http://joomla-flash.com/en/joomla-flash-menus/27-jf-blurry-joomla-flash-blur-effect-menu.html. A demo is also available here. This module can be used to display both horizontal and vertical menus.

More modules for displaying Flash menus on a Joomla! site are expected to be available soon.

Summary

Joomla! has a built-in menu management system that enables us to create multiple menus with many menu items. The menu management system in Joomla! is quite mature and easy to use. However, we may need to use Flash menus to make these menus look attractive. Flash menus may have several animation effects that prove to be nice for building more interactive websites. At the time of writing this book, very few extensions were available for adding Flash menus to a Joomla! site. However in this chapter, we have learned about two extensions that can help a website developer in adding Flash menus to Joomla!-based websites.

We have seen how to use the Flash Floating Menu module to add a menu with Flash animation effects. In this module we simply provided the menu icon images, links for these icons, tips for the icons, and finally, we published the module. There were also global configurations that we configured using the component.

We also saw the use of another commercially licensed extension, the Super Web Flash module for Joomla! 1.5. This is a multipurpose extension that can be used as a Flash header, a banner, and menu. There are many options to customize its appearance. We assigned the background images, links, and link texts. The module allows us to configure the manner in which the texts will be displayed along with its position. All these configurations are done from the **Parameters** section of the module.

With the ability to add Flash menus to our Joomla! site we will now be moving on to adding some Flash image galleries to our Joomla! website. The next chapter will show you how to build stunning photo galleries with Flash animation effects using some Joomla! extensions.

4
Creating Flash Photo Galleries

Up until now, we have seen how to use Joomla! extensions for displaying Flash animations and slideshows from a bunch of images. While creating slideshows from images, you might have thought about photo galleries. Photo galleries are common to many sites, especially Joomla!-based websites. Many components and modules are available for showing photo galleries. However, for achieving stunning Flash animation effects, you will need to use some extensions that can build and display photo galleries with Flash effects. In this chapter we are going to learn about such extensions for Joomla!. On the completion of this chapter, you will be able to:

- Describe some popular Joomla! extensions for building Flash photo galleries
- Build Flash photo galleries using Joomla! extensions such as Expose, Ozio Gallery, New Gallery, and Simple Flash Image Gallery

Although there are many extensions for showing Flash-based photo galleries, in this chapter we will discuss only the ones that are popular and are also freely available.

Building Flash photo galleries

There are several extensions in the Joomla! Extensions Directory for building Flash photo galleries, many of which are freely available. In fact, there are so many extensions in this category that choosing one from them may be a bit confusing. In this section, we will look into some of the popular extensions with non-commercial licensing. All these extensions can be freely downloaded from the Joomla! Extensions Directory.

Expose Flash Gallery

Expose Flash Gallery is probably the best available Flash photo gallery and it is widely used. It supports both Joomla! 1.0 and Joomla! 1.5. You can use this extension to build stunning photo and video galleries in a few minutes. You can download it for free from `http://joomlacode.org/gf/project/expose/frs/`. This link will take you to the file repository for the Expose Flash Gallery project on JoomlaCode. You will see many files listed there as shown in the following screenshot:

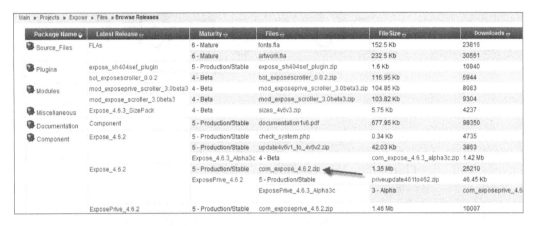

Package Name	Latest Release	Maturity	Files	File Size	Downloads
Source_Files	FLAs	6 - Mature	fonts.fla	152.5 Kb	23816
		6 - Mature	artwork.fla	232.5 Kb	30551
Plugins	expose_sh404sef_plugin	5 - Production/Stable	expose_sh404sef_plugin.zip	1.6 Kb	10940
	bot_exposescroller_0.0.2	4 - Beta	bot_exposescroller_0.0.2.zip	115.95 Kb	5944
Modules	mod_exposeprive_scroller_3.0beta3	4 - Beta	mod_exposeprive_scroller_3.0beta3.zip	104.85 Kb	8083
	mod_expose_scroller_3.0beta3	4 - Beta	mod_expose_scroller_3.0beta3.zip	103.82 Kb	9304
Miscellaneous	Expose_4.6.3_SizePack	4 - Beta	sizes_4v6v3.zip	5.75 Kb	4237
Documentation	Component	5 - Production/Stable	documentation1v6.pdf	677.95 Kb	98350
Component	Expose_4.6.2	5 - Production/Stable	check_system.php	0.34 Kb	4735
		5 - Production/Stable	update4v6v1_to_4v6v2.zip	42.03 Kb	3863
		Expose_4.6.3_Alpha3c 4 - Beta		com_expose_4.6.3_alpha3c.zip	1.42 Mb
	Expose_4.6.2	5 - Production/Stable	com_expose_4.6.2.zip	1.35 Mb	25210
		ExposePrive_4.6.2 5 - Production/Stable	priveupdate461to462.zip	46.45 Kb	
		ExposePrive_4.6.3_Alpha3c	3 - Alpha		com_exposeprive_4.6
	ExposePrive_4.6.2	5 - Production/Stable	com_exposeprive_4.6.2.zip	1.46 Mb	10007

From this list, first you need to install the `com_expose_4.6.2.zip` file for the Expose Flash Gallery component. Also download the module files, which are still in beta. If you are using the sh404sef component for building search engine-friendly URLs, then you also need to download the `expose_sh404sef_plugin.zip` file from the plugins section. It is also good to download the `documentation1v6.pdf` file. Note that one installation file works for both Joomla! 1.0 and Joomla! 1.5 (in legacy mode).

Like other Joomla! extensions, you can install this component too from **Extensions | Install/Uninstall**. Once installed, the component can be configured from the **Components | Expose** menu.

Configuring Expose gallery

Once you have installed the Expose gallery, you can start using the component without changing its default configuration. In fact, it has many configuration options, but the defaults are fine for most of the cases. Two types of settings can be configured: main settings and font settings.

To change the main settings, click on **Components | Expose | Configuration**. This brings up the **Expose 4 Configuration** screen shown in the following screenshot. You will see a lot of configuration fields on this screen.

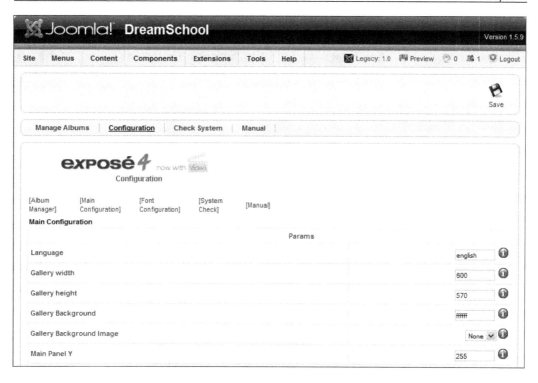

The screen lists the parameters on the left, and you can change these settings from the text fields in the right. In general, the settings are mainly for configuring the display of gallery, panels, albums, captions, and so on. The first few fields, such as **Gallery width**, **Gallery height**, **Gallery Background**, and **Gallery Background Image**, specify how the gallery will be displayed. You need to adjust the gallery's width and height according to the space available for displaying the component in the Joomla! template, through this screen. You can also specify a background color and an image for the gallery.

After defining the gallery settings, you can also define the settings for the main panel. You need to adjust the main panel's height, width, position, image buttons, and so on as per the space available in the template. You can also define settings for an image, such as its position from the top and the left. There are some other settings for the image also, such as the height and width of an image strip, settings for the image info box, slideshow, description, and so on. The fields are self-explanatory, and the values for these fields need to be entered based on your template design and the size of the images you are going to use in the photo gallery.

You can also configure the font for each section and items in the photo gallery. To configure the font settings, click on the **Font Configuration** link on the **Expose Configuration** screen. That shows the **Font Configuration** screen as shown in the following screenshot:

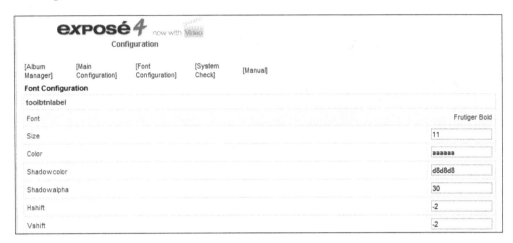

In the **Font Configuration** screen you can specify the font, font size, shadow color, shadow alpha, horizontal shift, vertical shift, and alignment for the screen items shown in the following table:

Screen Items	Description
toolbtnlabel	Set the mentioned settings for the label of a toolbar button.
label	You can specify the label's font settings from this section.
albumlist	Specify the font settings for the list of albums.
albumtitle	Specify the font settings for the title of an album.
imginfotitle	Specify the font settings for the title of an image information box.
imginfodate	Specify the font settings for the date shown in the image information box.
imginfolocation	Specify the font settings for the location shown in the image information box.
desc	Specify the font settings for the image description text.
albumnum	Specify the font settings for the album number.
selalblabel	Specify the font settings for the selected album's name
youarein	Specify the font settings for the path shown in 'you are in:' text.
imgstriptitle	Specify the font settings for the title of an image strip.
imgstripdateloc	Specify the font settings for the location of the image strip's date.
slideshowcountdown	Specify the font settings for the slideshow countdown number.

Screen Items	Description
Imgcounteridx	Specify the font settings for an image counter index.
imgcounterslash	Specify the font settings for the slash used in an image counter.
imgcountertotal	Specify the font settings for the image counter total.
helpguide	Specify the font settings for the help guide shown beside the album.
helptext	Specify the font settings for help text.
imgstripimgdesc	Specify the font settings for an image strip's description.
albuminfodescription	Specify font settings for an album's description
loadingalbum	Specify font settings for the text 'Loading...' displayed while the album is loading.
albumlistcancelbtn	Specify the font settings for the cancel button used for cancelling the album listing.
albumlistcancelbtn_ro	Specify the font settings for the cancel button shown in a row.

Most of the default font settings are acceptable for usual websites. However, you may need to change the font size, color, and other settings to match it to your site template.

> Due to a bug in the **Expose Configuration** screen, you see **Font** as fixed property reading **Frutiger Bold**. You cannot change this value from the administration panel. If you really want to change the font settings (font name), you need to edit the `./components/com_expose/expose/config/formats.xml` file. You can change the font name inside the `<font> </font>` tag in this file.

Creating collections and albums

Collections and albums are created using the **Album Manager**. You can start the **Album Manager** by clicking on **Components | Expose | Manage Albums**. By default, the Expose Album Manager is password protected, and the default password for accessing it as a manager is *manager*. On clicking **Components | Expose | Manage Albums**, you will see a login screen as shown in the following screenshot:

Type the default password (*manager*) in the **Password** field and click on the **Log in** button. You can change the password after logging in. To avoid typing the password every time, select the **Save** checkbox. Once you are logged in, you will see the list of albums, photos and, videos, as shown in the following screenshot:

You can create collections and albums and add photos and videos to these albums from this screen. The box on the left shows the list of collections and albums. As you see, albums can remain under a collection or even outside them. When you select an album from the list, photos and videos in that album are listed in the **Photos and videos** box. When you select an album, you also see the thumbnail for the album and its description in the **Description** textbox. Selecting an image or a video from the list shows its description in **Description** textbox below the list.

To create a new collection, click on the **Create collection** button. That shows the **Create collection** dialog as shown in the next screenshot:

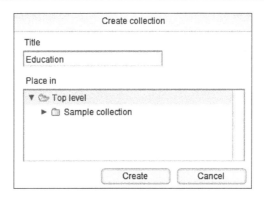

Type the title of the collection, and select its parent collection. If this is the top collection, then select **Top level** from the list and click on the **Create** button. This adds the collection.

The difference between a collection and an album is that a collection is a container for albums and cannot hold images or videos. You need to create albums for adding photos and videos. To create an album, click on the **Create album** button. That shows the **Create album** dialog box shown in the following screenshot:

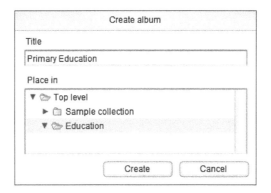

This is similar to the **Create collection** dialog box. Type in the title of the album, and select its parent collection from the list. Then, click on the **Create** button to add the album to the selected collection.

Similar to the collection, an album can also be created at the top level without having a parent collection. However, you cannot create an album under another album. You can create as many albums you need under a collection. You can rename or delete the collection and albums at any time. To rename a collection or an album, select that collection or an album and click on the **Rename** button. That shows the **Rename Collection** or **Rename Album** dialog. Type the new name of the collection or album and click on the **Rename** button in the dialog box.

Besides renaming a collection or an album, you can also delete a collection or an album. To do so, simply select the collection or album and click on the **Delete** button. That shows a confirmation dialog box, and once you have clicked **Yes** in the confirmation dialog, the selected collection/album will be deleted.

 Deleting a collection will delete all the albums and photos and videos in the albums, too. Therefore, be careful when deleting a collection or an album. If you need to keep an album and want to put it inside another collection, you must move it before deleting the collection.

Generally, the collections and albums are displayed in the order in which they were created. However, you can change the order of the albums. Select a collection or album and click on the **Up** or **Down** button to change the order.

Adding photos and videos to albums

Once collections and albums have been created, you can upload the photos and videos to the album. To upload the photos to an album, select the album and click on the **Upload photos** button. That shows the **Upload photos** dialog box shown in the following screenshot:

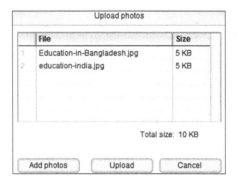

Click on the **Add photos** button on the **Upload photos** dialog box and select the photos you want to upload. The names and the sizes of the selected photos will be displayed in this dialog box. Once you have added the required number of photos, click on the **Upload** button. Uploading of the photos will start and it will continue for some time depending on the number of photos selected and the speed of the connection to the internet. On successful upload you will be notified about the success. Click on **OK** in this **Success** dialog box, and you will be taken to the **Album Manager** screen again. Now, select the album where you have uploaded the photos and the list of photos will be displayed in the **Photos and videos** box. Clicking on the name of a photo will display its preview in the box below it, as shown in the following screenshot:

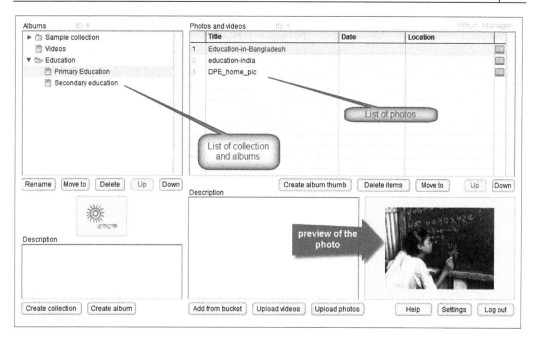

To add or edit any text in the **Photos and videos** box, double-click on the text or field (for example, the **Date** field) and enter the text for that field. You can specify a title, date, and location for each photo that you have uploaded. Among the photos uploaded, you can use one as the thumbnail for the album. To use a photo as thumbnail for the album, select the photo title and click on the **Create album thumb** button. That shows the **Create album or collection thumbnail** dialog box shown in the next screenshot:

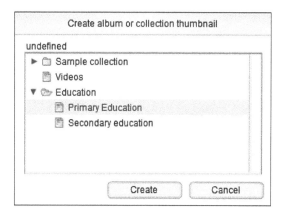

Select an album or a collection from the list in the **Create album or collection thumbnail** dialog box (for example, **Primary Education**), and click on the **Create** button to create the thumbnail from the selected photo. A thumbnail is created and whenever you select the album or collection, the thumbnail will be displayed.

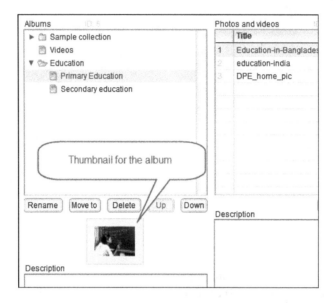

You can also upload Flash videos to an album. To upload a Flash video (.flv file) to an album, select the album and click on the **Upload videos** button. That brings up the **Upload photos** dialog box shown in the following screenshot:

From the browse dialog box, select the Flash video (.flv) file you want to upload. The list of Flash video files will be displayed in the **Upload photos** dialog box. Now click on the **Upload** button and the selected videos will be uploaded to the album. On completion of the upload you will be notified by the **Success** dialog box. Click on **OK** on the **Success** dialog box, and you will be taken to **Album Manager** screen. Now you should see the name of the video that you have uploaded. Select the video and a preview of the video will be displayed below the box, as shown in the following screenshot:

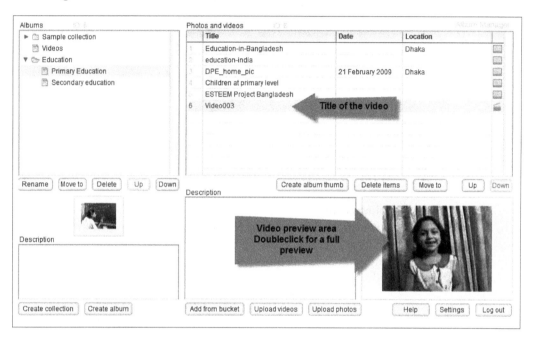

Double-click the preview area (shown by a marker in the screenshot) to view a bigger photo or video preview. For video preview, you can run the full preview of the video and also capture a thumbnail image from the video. Double-clicking on the **Video preview** area will show a preview of the video as shown in the following screenshot:

It is good to preview the full video after uploading it to the album. You can see the video and hear the audio from such a preview.

You can rearrange the photos and videos added to the album similarly to the albums. Select a photo or a video from the list and click on the **Up** or **Down** button to fix its position. Similarly, you can select a photo or video and click on the **Move to** button to move the photo or video to another album. For deleting an item, select that item and click on the **Delete items** button.

You can also specify some settings for uploading photos and videos. Click on the **Settings** button just below the preview area. That shows the **Settings** dialog box shown in the following screenshot:

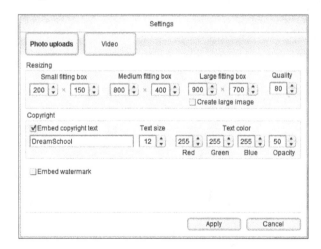

In this dialog box, click on **Photo Uploads**, and you will see the settings for uploading a photo to an album. It has mainly two groups of settings: **Resizing** and **Copyright**. In the **Resizing** section you can specify the size of **Small fitting box**, **Medium fitting box**, and **Large fitting box**. You can also specify an acceptable quality degradation for resizing. If you want to create a larger image from one smaller image, select the **Create larger image** checkbox.

In the **Copyright** section, select the **Embed copyright text** and type the text to be embedded to the image, for example, DreamSchool. Then specify **Text size** and **Text color** with **Opacity**. You can also check **Embed watermark** to add the Expose logo as watermark to the image. The following screenshot demonstrates the effect of embedding copyright text and a watermark:

 The watermark and the copyright information will be embedded to the images uploaded after the settings have been changed. Changing the configurations, that is enabling the watermark and the copyright text, will not cause them be applied to the already uploaded image files. They will be added to the newly uploaded files only.

In the **Settings** dialog box, you can specify the upload settings for videos by clicking on the **Video** button. That shows the settings for videos as shown in the following screenshot:

There are only two settings for video uploads: the size of the thumbnail and its quality. Specify the optimal **Size** and **Quality** for the video thumbnail from this dialog box.

Showing the album

Showing albums on the Joomla! frontend is straightforward. You simply create a menu link to the Expose component, and the users can access the component using this link. For creating a menu link, from the Joomla! administration panel, click on **Menus | Main Menu | New**, then click on **Expose**. You get the **Menu Item: [New]** screen like the one shown in the following screenshot:

Provide a **Title** for the menu item and an **Alias** to be used for an SEF URL. From the **Display in** drop-down list, select the menu where the link is to be added. You can also select a parent item for this from the **Parent Item** listbox. Check **Yes** in the **Published** field. Now, define an access level: select **Public** to make the galleries publicly accessible, otherwise select **Registered** or **Special** from the **Access Level** listbox. From the **Parameters (System)** section you can specify a title and a suffix for the page. Save the menu item and preview the site. You will find the menu item on the frontend. Clicking on a menu item, for example, **Expose Gallery**, you will see the list of available collections and albums as shown in the following screenshot:

As you can see, the number of items in the album is also displayed besides the album name. But for the collection, we see an arrow. Clicking on this arrow will display the albums available within the collection. Further, clicking on the album you will see the photos and videos in it as shown in this screenshot:

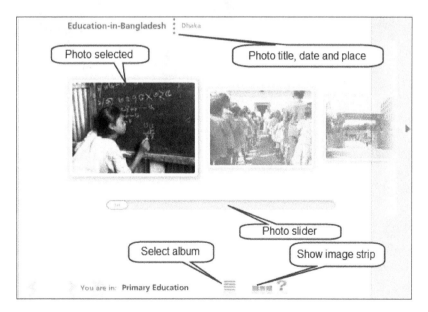

As can be seen from the screenshot, the images are displayed in an image strip. Whenever you hover your mouse pointer on an image, that image becomes highlighted and its information (title, date, and place) is displayed above the image strip. There is a photo slider with which you can view the other images in the strip quickly. Below the photo slider, you see the main control panel for the image strip and album selection. You can select another album from this and can also view the current location. To view the full image, click on the image shown in the image strip. Doing so displays the full image as shown in the following screenshot:

While viewing the full image, the previous, next, and slideshow buttons are active. You can view a slideshow by clicking on the slideshow button. You can return to image strip-view at anytime by clicking on the show image strip icon.

Showing the Expose Scroller module

Another way of showing Expose photo galleries is using the Scroller module for Expose. The Expose Thumbnail Scroller module is freely available for download from `http://joomlacode.org/gf/project/expose/frs/`. Download the `mod_expose_scroller_3.0beta3.zip` file from the above mentioned URL, and install this module from the **Extensions | Install/Uninstall** screen. Once it is installed, you will see the **Expose Thumbnail Scroller** module listed in the **Extensions | Module Manager** screen. Click on this module, and you will see the **Module: [Edit]** screen. Provide a title for the module and publish it. Now, preview the site, and you will find the scrolling Expose thumbnail module as shown in the following screenshot:

While publishing the module, you can specify what should be displayed if an image shown in the module is clicked on. You can choose to display the respective album, photo, or collection. You can even disable linking the photos to anything.

 Linking images shown in the **Expose Image Scroller** module works fine with non-SEF URLs. When you are using **search-engine friendly** (**SEF**) URLs, the linking to albums, photos, and collection does not work. If you are using sh404sef extension for an SEF URL, there is a workaround. You can download and use expose_sh404sef_plugin from http://joomlacode.org/gf/project/expose/frs/.

Using the Expose plugin

For adding any album or photo in the content from the Expose photo gallery, there is a plugin called Expose Scroller. Visit http://joomlacode.org/gf/project/expose/frs/ and download the bot_exposescroller_0.0.2.zip file. Install the plugin, and you will find the plugin name Expose Scroller in the **Extensions | Plugin Manager** screen. Click on this plugin, and you get the **Plugin: [Edit]** screen as show in the following screenshot:

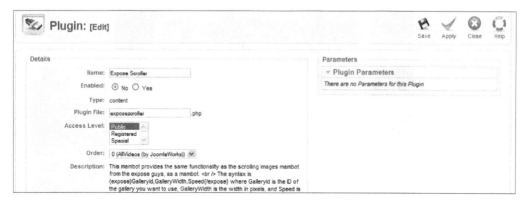

Enable the plugin and read the instructions for using it. The syntax for using this plugin is very simple:

```
{expose}GalleryId,GalleryWidth,Speed{/expose}
```

You need to specify the gallery ID, gallery width in pixels, and speed. Speed is simply a number; the greater the value, the lower will be the speed. We can embed a gallery in any Joomla! content by using code like the following:

```
{expose}7,600px,2{/expose}
```

With the plugin enabled, and existence of a gallery with ID 7, the gallery will be displayed inside the content.

Ozio Gallery

Ozio Gallery is a photo gallery that displays photos from a folder in a 3D Flash-based photo gallery. It can show the photos from your Flickr account as well. The details of Ozio Gallery and its download link can be found at `http://extensions.joomla.org/extensions/4883/details`.

Download the component from this link and install it from the **Extensions | Install/Uninstall** screen. Once installed, just create a menu link to the Ozio Gallery component so that you can access the component. After adding the menu item and clicking on it, the photo gallery will look as shown in the following screenshot:

If you see a black screen in the gallery, it is because you have nothing to show in the gallery. Please follow the steps described in the following sections, configure the image sources, and then try again to see the gallery images.

One of the great things about Ozio Gallery is that you get 3D Flash animation instantly, by default, without configuring anything. The only thing is that you have to put the photos in its directory, which is set to `images/oziogallery` by default. It has another great feature of showing photos from your Flickr account.

After installing the Ozio Gallery, you can configure this component by selecting **Components | Ozio Gallery**. That shows the description and credits for it. The actual configuration is done by clicking on the **Settings** button in the toolbar.

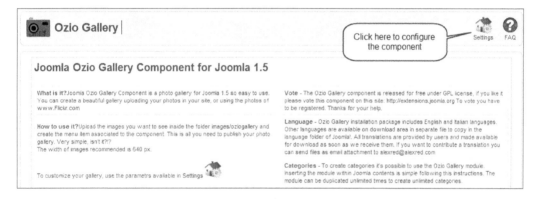

Now we will look into how to configure the Ozio Gallery and display photos from your Flickr account or from a folder on the web server.

Showing photos from Flickr

If you have uploaded photos to your account at Flickr (www.flickr.com), you can show those photos inside Ozio Gallery. To configure Ozio Gallery, click on **Components | Ozio Gallery** and then click on the **Settings** button in the toolbar. That shows the **Ozio Gallery - Settings** screen.

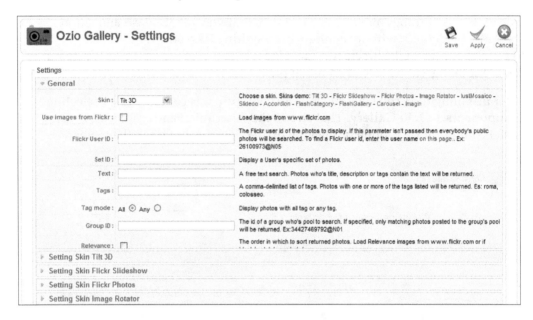

As you can see, the **Ozio Gallery – Settings** screen has several sections for configuring the different aspects of the gallery. First we will see the **General** section, from where we can set the skin and choose whether we want to display images from a Flickr account.

First you need to choose a skin. There are several skins available with Ozio Gallery. Out of these Tilt 3D, Flickr Sildeshow, Flickr Photos, and Flickr Slideoo skins are suitable for use with photos from Flickr. On the other hand, Tilt 3D, Image Rotator, LustMosaico, Accordion, FlashCategory, FlashGallery, Corousel, and Imagin are suitable for displaying photos from a folder. We will be looking into these skins and their settings later.

If you want to display the photos from your Flickr account, configure the following fields in the **General** section:

- **Skin**: From this drop-down list, select a skin suitable for displaying Flickr photos. You can select Tilt 3D, Flickr Slideshows, Flickr Photos, or Flickr Slideoo for displaying the photos on Flickr.

- **Use images from Flickr**: Select this checkbox to display Flickr images. Once it is checked, you can set the values for the fields following it.

- **Flickr User ID**: Enter your Flickr User ID in this field. Remember that the Flickr User ID is different from the login name used for logging into Flickr. You can find the Flickr User ID by clicking on the link provided to the right of this field or by visiting http://www.flickr.com/services/api/explore/?method=flickr.people.findByUsername, shown in the following screenshot, and typing the login name. A Flickr User ID generally looks like 27545167@N00.

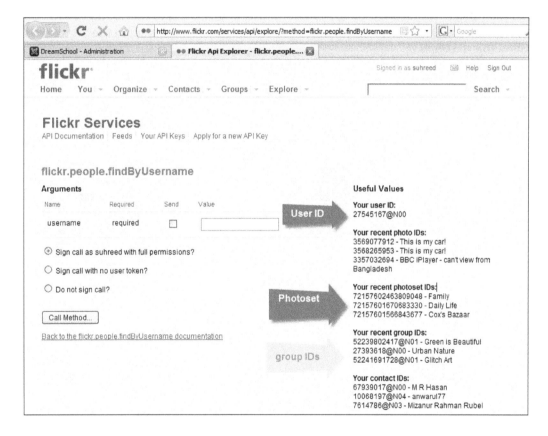

- **Set ID**: You can specify the **Set ID** to display a specific set of photos. Once you have logged into your Flickr account and visited the above URL, you can see the photoset IDs and the Group IDs too.

- **Text**: You can specify some search text for displaying images relevant to those keywords. For example, we can specify beach, Bangladesh, and nature as search keywords.

- **Tags**: You can specify tags to be searched for the photos in Flickr.

- **Tag mode**: Specify whether all or any of the tags mentioned in the earlier field should be searched for. If you select **All** in this field, only the photos matching all of the above tags will be displayed.

- **Group ID**: If you have participated in any Flickr group, you can specify the ID of that group in this field so that photos are searched for in that group too.

- **Relevance**: Select this checkbox to ensure that search results are sorted as per their relevance to the search keywords.

For example, I want to display my Flickr photos in this gallery. Therefore, I have configured the **Ozio Gallery - Settings | General** section as shown in the following screenshot:

When these settings are saved and previewed, Ozio Gallery will look as shown in the following screenshot:

OzioGallery by Joomla.it

As you can see, when you hover your mouse pointer over the photo, a list of the photos is displayed below the main photo. On the top you will see the controls for the slideshow, from where you can view the previous or the next photo and adjust the slideshow speed.

Showing photos from a folder

Displaying images from Flickr is a good idea. However, you may also need to show your images that have been kept in a folder on the web server. Ozio Gallery provides you skins to display the photos from a folder. To do so, in the **General** section, deselect the **Use images from Flickr** checkbox and select a skin appropriate for displaying images from a folder. For example, you have selected **LustMosaico** as the skin. Now go to the **Setting Skin LustMosaico** section as shown in the following screenshot:

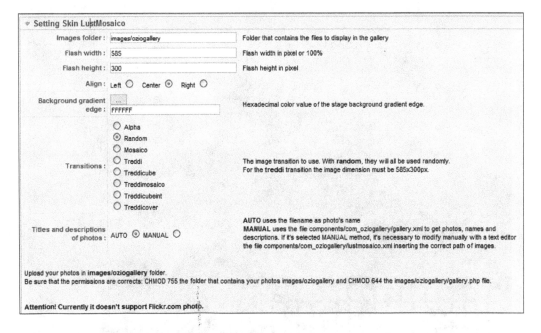

In the **Setting Skin LustMosaico** screen first, you need to configure the **Images folder** with the location from where the images will be displayed. The default location for storing images for Ozio Gallery is `images/oziogallery`. If you want to change the location, then specify the directory path in the **Images folder** field.

The default path for uploading gallery images is `images/oziogallery`; this is where you need to upload your photos. If you want to use some other directory, it should have the appropriate permissions. For example, on a Linux server the images folder should have a chmod value of 755.

You can specify the width and the height of the gallery in the **Flash width** and the **Flash height** fields respectively. You may need to adjust these values to fit into your site template. You can also set the alignment, background gradient, and transitions. There are several transitions available for this (LustMosaico) skin. You can select each of them one by one and see the result, then finally set the transition of your choice. The title and description of the images can be set either automatically or manually. If **Auto** is chosen in **Titles and descriptions of photos**, the image names will be used as title. You can set both the image title and the descriptions manually through the `components/com_oziogallery/gallery.xml` file. The file describes each image in the following format:

```
<tiltviewergallery>
 <photos>
   <photo imageurl="http://exemple.xx/images/oziogallery/img.jpg">
      <title>Image 1</title>
      <description>
         This is a regular text description.
      </description>
   </photo>
   <photo imageurl="http://exemple.xx/images/oziogallery/img.jpg">
   <title>Image 2</title>
   <description>
   <![CDATA[This is a HTML text description. Supported tags are
      <b>bold</b>, <u>underline</u>, <i>italics</i>,
      linebreaks<br>and <font color="#ff0000" size="60">
      font tags</font>. Hyperlinks are not supported.]]>
   </description>
   </photo>
 </photos>
</tiltviewergallery>
```

You need to edit this `gallery.xml` file manually through a text editor to add the image titles, image URLs, and descriptions. Although the `gallery.xml` file contains image URLs, the LustMosaic skin uses the image path from another file named `components/com_oziogallery/lustmosaic.xml`. Locations of the images are defined in this file as shown here:

```
<?xml version="1.0" encoding="UTF-8"?>
<tiltviewergallery>
<photos>
   <photo>
    <location>
       http://www.exemple.xx/images/oziogallery/001.jpg
    </location>
   </photo>
```

```
<photo>
 <location>
    http://www.exemple.xx/images/oziogallery/002.jpg
 </location>
</photo>
<photo>
 <location>
    http://www.exemple.xx/images/oziogallery/003.jpg
 </location>
</photo>
</photos>
</tiltviewergallery>
```

Remember that, for the image title and description, LustMosaic skin still depends on the `gallery.xml` file. Therefore, you need to modify both the `gallery.xml` and `lustmosaic.xml` files manually.

Once all the fields for LustMosaic skin have been configured, save the settings and preview Ozio Gallery in the site's frontend. The photo gallery will look as shown in the following screenshot:

As you can see, the images are now being shown from the specified folder, that is `images/oziogallery`. Whenever you add new images to that directory, those images will also be displayed in the photo gallery.

Configuration for skins

We have used the Flickr Slideshow and LustMosaic skins in the two examples discussed so far. However, you can use any other skin suitable for the kind of images being displayed. For example, you can select Tilt 3D, Image Rotator, Accordion, FlashCategory, FlashGallery, Carousel, or Imagin for showing images from a directory, whereas other skins can be used for displaying images from Flickr. For each of these skins, you can configure the settings. Now we will look into the configuration options for each of these skins.

Tilt 3D skin

The Tilt 3D skin can be used for displaying the images from either a folder or Flickr. This is the default skin used for Ozio Gallery. Once you have chosen Tilt 3D in the **General** section, you need to configure its settings for from the **Setting Skin Tilt 3D** section.

The first thing that you need to do is to configure the **Images folder** to the location from which the images will be displayed in the photo gallery. By default, this field reads the path as `images/oziogallery`, which is fine for most cases. You have to upload all your images to this folder and these will be automatically displayed in the photo gallery. However, when Tilt 3D has been selected as the skin and the **Use images from Flickr** checkbox in the **General** section is selected, this field will be ignored and the images from Flickr will be displayed instead.

After the path of **Images folder**, you can specify the height and width of the Flash gallery. This can be specified in pixels or as percentage. Also, set the alignment for the Flash gallery. Then, set the number of columns and rows for displaying the images. You can set the background gradient color, frame color, back color, and so on from this section.

We can enable downloading of images from our image galleries. To do so, select the **Enable download/link mode** checkbox, and in the **Button Text** field, type **Download**. Then, for each image in the `images/oziogallery` directory, you need to create a ZIP file and put that file in the `images/oziogallery/files` directory. For example, if you have an image named `primary_school_classroom.png` in the `images/oziogallery` directory, then you need to compress that image and save it in the `images/oziogallery/files` directory as `primary_school_classroom.zip`. The download link will be displayed in the images backside, when viewed in the photo gallery, and by clicking on the download link, users will get the `.zip` file of that image.

In the **Photo Description** field, you can type a line of text that will be used as a description for all the images. If you want to use a separate description for each image, you need to select **Manual** in the **Titles and Descriptions of Photos** field and edit the `components/com_oziogallery/gallery.xml` file, whose structure has been shown earlier.

When it has been selected it in **General** section and has been properly configured, a photo gallery with Tilt 3D skin will look like the one shown in the following screenshot:

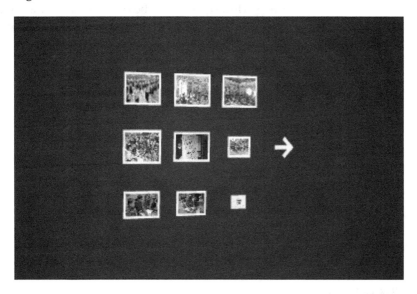

The image list will be tilted to left or right on the movement of the mouse. Move your mouse pointer over the image thumbnails and you see the tilting effect. To view the full image, click on one image. The image will look bigger as shown in the following screenshot:

Click here to see the Reverse

As you see, the image becomes larger when you click on its thumbnail.
Also note the rotate icon displayed at the bottom-right of the image. Clicking on this button will show you the reverse side of the image. If you have added a description for the image, the image description will be displayed on the reverse. If downloading is enabled, a download link will also be visible. This is shown in the following screenshot:

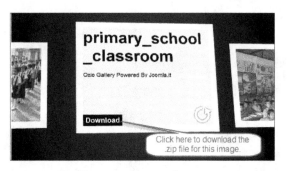

Clicking on the **Download** link will download the image's `.zip` file to the user's computer. Clicking again on the rotate icon will show the front side of the image.

Flickr Slideshow skin

The Flickr Slideshow skin is for displaying images from Flickr (`www.flickr.com`). This does not show images from the `images` folder on your web server. Once the skin is selected in the **General** section, the **Use images from Flickr** checkbox is selected, and Flickr-related settings have been configured, this skin will display the slideshow with images taken from Flickr as shown in the following screenshot:

You don't need to configure any settings for this skin, except the settings for Flickr in the **General** section. It can use the Flickr User ID, the photoset ID, tags, text searches, and the Group ID configured in the **General** section.

Flickr Photos skin

Flickr Photos is another skin for showing images from Flickr. This skin doesn't show images from a web server's folder. You don't need to configure this skin separately, but you do need to select the **Use images from Flickr** checkbox in the **General** section along with the other settings related to Flickr. When this skin is selected in the **General** section and the other settings for Flickr are configured, the gallery will look like the one shown in the following screenshot:

No extra settings are needed for using the Flickr Photos skin.

Image Rotator skin

The Image Rotator skin can display images from a web server's folder or images from Flickr. When this skin is selected in the **General** section and the information regarding Flickr is provided, this skin displays images from Flickr. When Flickr is disabled, this screen displays images from the local folder configured in the **Configure Skin Image Rotator** section. The following screenshot shows the **Configure Skin Image Rotator** section:

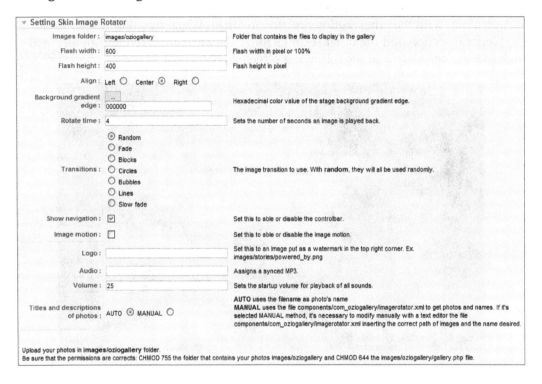

From the **Setting Skin Image Rotator** screen you can configure the path to the images folder, the width and height of the gallery, the alignment, the image motion, and how titles and descriptions will be used. If you choose to use titles and descriptions manually, you need to configure the image names and paths in the `components/com_oziogallery/imagerotator.xml` file. The structure of this file is as follows:

```xml
<?xml version="1.0" encoding="utf-8"?>
<tiltviewergallery>
   <photos>
      <track>
         <title>Image 1</title>
         <location>
            http://exemple.xx/images/oziogallery/img.jpg
         </location>
         <info>
            http://www.joomla.it
         </info>
      </track>
      ...
   </photos>
</tiltviewergallery>
```

Once configured properly, this skin will display the photo gallery as shown in this screenshot:

LustMosaico skin

This skin is used to display photos from a local folder only. It does not support Flickr photos yet. We have already seen how to configure and use this skin to display photos from a specified folder.

Flickr Slideoo

The Flickr Slideoo skin is used for displaying slideshow with images from Flickr. To use this skin, select it from **General** section, enable using Flickr images, provide the Flickr User ID, and then configure the skin from the **Setting Skin Flickr Slideoo** section as shown in the following screenshot:

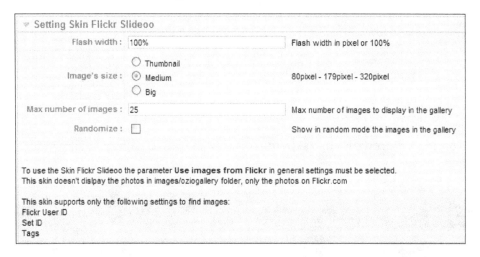

From the **Setting Skin Flickr Slideoo** screen you can configure the width of the Flash gallery, the image size, and the maximum number of images to be displayed. You can enable **Randomize** to show images in a random order.

When chosen and configured properly, the Flickr Slideoo skin will display the photo gallery as shown in the following screenshot:

Accordion skin

If you have used modern JavaScript frameworks or the so-called Web 2.0 designs, you may know what an *accordion effect* is. The Accordion skin in Ozio Gallery creates the same accordion effect and displays the images from the local folder specified. You can configure its settings from the **Setting Skin Accordion** section as shown in the following screenshot:

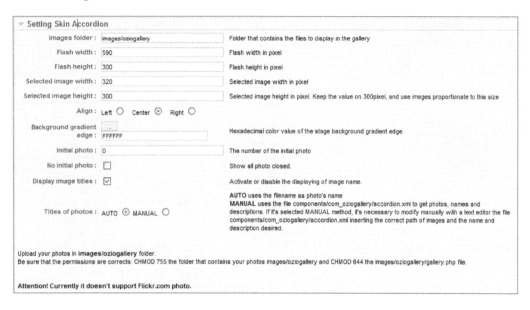

Like other skins, here too you can specify the images folder where the images will be stored and displayed from. You can also configure the gallery's height and width, alignment, the height and width of a selected image, and the number of initial photos. You can add image titles and descriptions manually by editing the `components/com_oziogallery/accordion.xml` file. Once enabled and configured properly, this skin will show the photo gallery as shown in the following screenshot:

With this skin you see the names of the images listed vertically—like the books kept in a bookshelf. When you click on a name, you will see the image.

FlashCategory skin

The FlashCategory skin is used to display images from a folder. It has a unique feature compared to other skins—you simply put the images in subfolders in the `images` folder, say `images/oziogallery/`, and the FlashCategory skin displays each subfolder as one category. You can configure this skin from the **Setting Skin FlashCatergoy** screen as shown in the following screenshot:

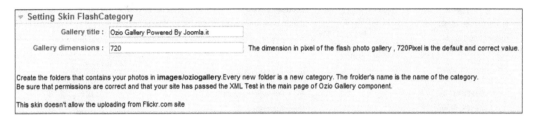

As you see, you can set the gallery title and dimensions for this skin. This skin can only show images from the `images` folder and its subfolders, not from Flickr.

When enabled and configured properly, the photo gallery with this skin will look like the one shown in the following screenshot:

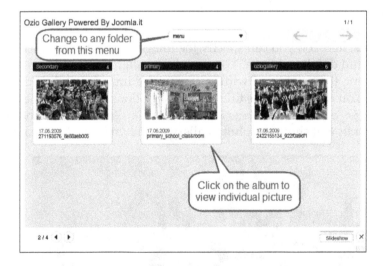

As shown in the screenshot, there are three folders in the photo gallery. You can change over to any folder by selecting the folder from the menu or by directly clicking on the folder thumbnail. You can then view the images in that category as a slideshow.

FlashGallery skin

The FlashGallery skin can be used for displaying images from either a local folder or Flickr. It searches for images from Flickr by using the **Flickr User ID** set in the **General** section. You can configure this skin from the **Setting Skin FlashGallery** screen shown in the following screenshot:

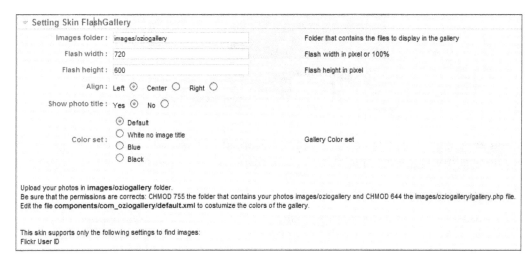

If this skin is selected in the **General** section and the **Use images from Flickr** field is unchecked, then this skin displays images from the location configured in the **Images folder** field. You can also configure the gallery's height, width, alignment, and color set from this configuration screen.

Once enabled and configured properly, a photo gallery with this skin will look like the one shown in the following screenshot:

If you are using images from Flickr, captions are also displayed with the image. For images from a folder, image names are displayed as caption.

Carousel skin

The Carousel skin is for displaying images from a folder. It cannot display images from Flickr. You can configure this skin from the **Setting Skin Carousel** section shown in the following screenshot:

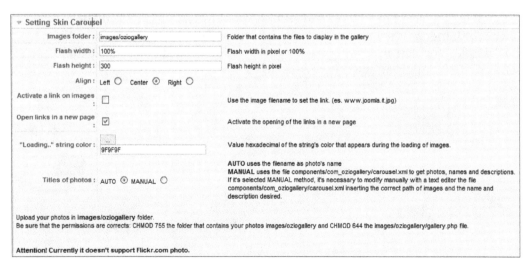

As you see, you can set the images folder, the width, the height, the alignment of the Flash gallery, and activate a link on images, if you want to. You can also set how the title of photos should be displayed. Like other skins, Carousel skin too uses a `.xml` file to get the photo location, title, and descriptions. It takes this information from the `components/com_oziogallery/carousel.xml` file. You can link an image to a particular URL. To do so, select the **Activate a link on images** checkbox and rename the filenames after the domain you want to link. For example, for linking an image to `www.bnfe.gov.bd`, the image name should be `www.bnfe.gov.bd.png`.

When enabled and configured properly, photo galleries with this skin will look like the one shown in the following screenshot:

As you can see in this screenshot, this skin produces a nice effect. When you move your mouse pointer, the images will rotate too.

Imagin skin

The Imagin skin can display images from a folder and also those from Flickr. You can configure its settings from the **Setting Skin Imagin** section as shown in the following screenshot:

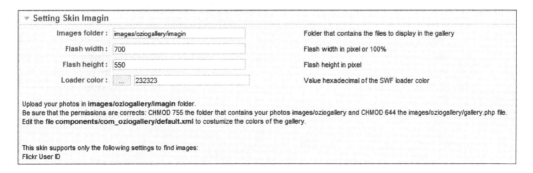

Like the other skin settings, you can also set the images folder, the Flash gallery width, the height, and the loader color in the **Setting Skin Imagin** section. By default, the `images/oziogallery/imagin` folder is used for storing images. You can change this folder, but you have to copy the `images/oziogallery/imagin/_preferences.xml` file into the new folder you are referring to. You need to upload your images in the folder specified in the **Images folder** field.

Once the skin is enabled and configured properly, a photo gallery with this skin will look as shown in the following screenshot:

The Imagin skin produces nice slideshows. You can view the images in the normal view by clicking on the **Normal View** link. Clicking on **FullScreen** will display a slideshow occupying the whole screen. At the bottom you will see the timeline. Taking the mouse pointer over this timeline displays the thumbnails of the images.

Version 2.x of Ozio Gallery is somehow different from the version 1.0.9 discussed in this book. In version 2.x, you will not find the **Settings** screen, instead you have to configure the gallery display from the **Parameters** section while creating a menu link. During the creation of a menu link to Ozio Gallery2, you have to choose the skin you want to use. Based on the skin chosen, you will get a set of parameters similar to the **Settings** options discussed in this chapter. The latest version of Ozio Gallery can be downloaded from `http://code.google.com/p/oziogallery2/downloads/list`.

New Gallery

New Gallery is a simple but powerful Flash image gallery. It takes images from your web server and displays them as a Flash gallery. You can also add categories to the images. This component is freely available from `http://www.webmaster-tips.net/Download/View-details/9-Joomla-Components/176-New-Gallery-Flash-Image-Gallery.html`.

Once it is downloaded and installed from the **Extensions | Install/Uninstall** screen, you can configure the component from the **Components | New Gallery | Configuration** screen shown in the following screenshot:

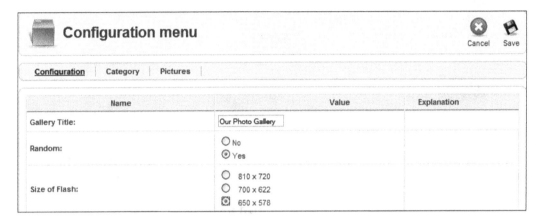

In the **Configuration Menu** screen you need to provide a title for the gallery, set whether images will be shown randomly or not, and select the size of the Flash gallery from the three given choices: **810 x 720**, **700 x 622**, and **650 x 578**. Click on the **Category** link on this screen and you get the **Category menu** screen shown in the following screenshot:

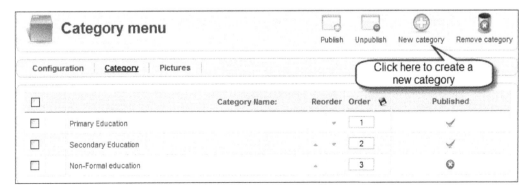

The **Category menu** screen will list existing categories. You can publish, unpublish, or remove categories from this screen. To create a new category click on the **New category** button in the toolbar. You will get a form where you must enter a name for the new category and then click on the **New Category** button.

To add pictures to the gallery click on the **Pictures** link or select **Components | New Gallery | Pictures**. This shows the **Pictures menu** screen shown in the next screenshot. This screen lists the existing pictures that have been uploaded to the gallery:

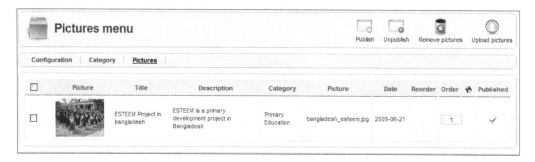

You can publish, unpublish, or remove any picture by selecting that picture in the **Pictures menu** screen and clicking on the **Publish, Unpublish,** or **Remove pictures** buttons respectively on the toolbar. You can also upload pictures by clicking on the **Upload pictures** button. Clicking on the **Upload pictures** button shows another screen for uploading pictures as shown in the following screenshot:

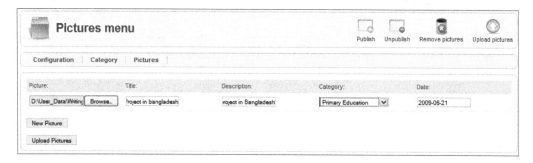

In this screen, click on the **Browse** button and select the picture to be uploaded, give a title and a description for the picture, choose a category, and provide the date for the picture. For each picture to be uploaded, click on the **New Picture** button and fill in the same row of information. Then, click on the **Upload Pictures** button to start uploading the pictures on your web server. Once you are done with uploading, the pictures, along with their thumbnails, will be listed in the **Pictures menu** screen as shown in the following screenshot:

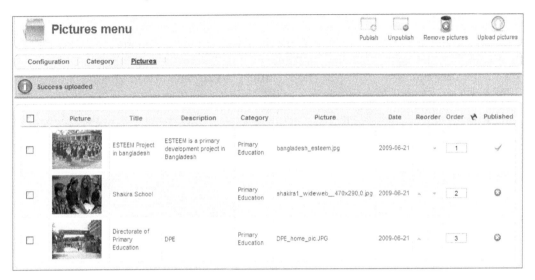

For viewing the photo gallery created by the New Gallery component, create a menu item on main menu or any other menu. Choose a link to this **New Gallery** component. The users can then access the gallery through that menu item. When the gallery is configured and the pictures have been uploaded, it may look as shown in the following screenshot:

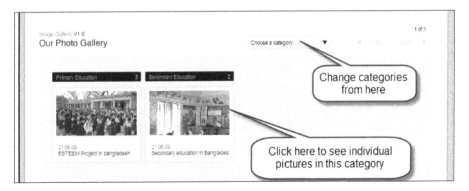

You can upload pictures from the Joomla! administration panel. However, this component displays a link to the developer's site. Another limitation is that once an image is added, you cannot edit its title and description.

Simple Flash Image Gallery (SFIG)

Simple Flash Image Gallery (SFIG) is yet another freely available Flash-based image gallery. You can download it from `http://www.webmaster-tips.net/Download/ View-details/9-Joomla-Components/175-Simple-Flash-Image-Gallery- SFIG-j15.html` by registering to the website. Once downloaded and installed from the **Extensions | Install/Uninstall** screen, you can configure this component by selecting **Components | _Simple Flash Gallery | Configuration**. This shows the **Configuration menu** screen as shown in the following screenshot:

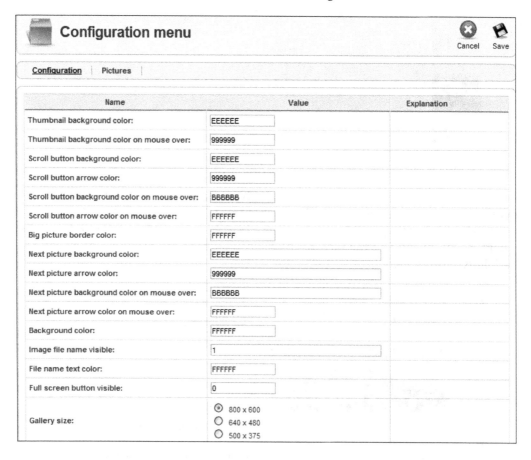

From the **Configuration menu** screen you can set the thumbnail background color, the border size, the scroll button color, and so on. You can also choose the gallery size from the three given options: **800 x 600**, **640 x 480**, and **500 x 375** pixels.

Once the configurations are set, click on the **Pictures** link or select **Components | _Simple Flash Gallery | Pictures**. You will see the existing images in the gallery listed in the **Pictures menu** screen as shown in the following screenshot:

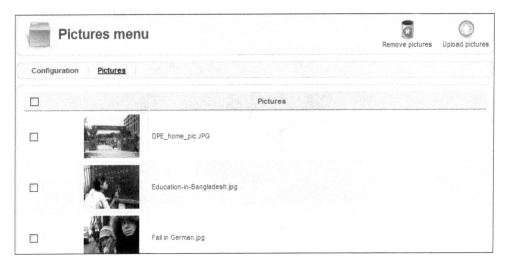

For uploading pictures to this gallery, click on the **Upload pictures** button on the toolbar. This brings up a form from where you can select the pictures that you want to upload, shown in the following screenshot:

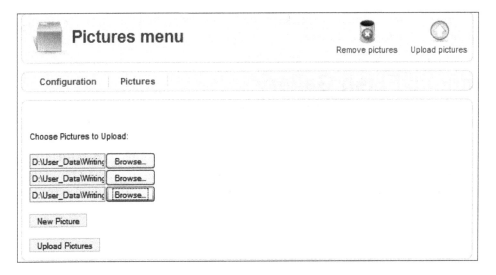

In this form, click on the **Browse** button and select the picture to be uploaded. To add another picture, click on the **New Picture** button. Select as many pictures as you want to upload and finally, click on the **Upload Pictures** button. The pictures will be uploaded to your web server soon.

Like other gallery components, you also need to create a menu item for Simple Flash Gallery, so that the users can access the gallery from the frontend. When accessed from the frontend, the gallery will look as shown in the following screenshot:

As you can see, in this gallery you cannot view a slideshow, you can only view images one by one. You need to click on the left or the right arrow or click on the thumbnails below to see a picture.

Dynamic Flash Gallery

Dynamic Flash Gallery is another simple image gallery that uses Flash effects. This is available for free at http://www.webmaster-tips.net/Download/View-details/9-Joomla-Components/180-Dynamic-Flash-Gallery-for-Joomla-1.5.html. Once downloaded and installed from the **Extensions | Install/Uninstall** screen, you can configure this component by selecting **Components | Dynamic Flash Gallery | Config Dynamic Gallery**. This shows the **Config menu** screen as shown in the following screenshot:

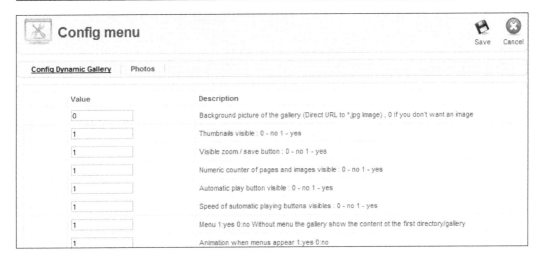

In the **Config menu** screen you will see the field description to the right and its value in the left column. Change these values as needed. To upload pictures to the gallery, click on the **Photos** link or select **Components | Dynamic Flash Gallery | Photos**. This shows the **Config menu** screen and asks you to choose a gallery. Select a gallery from the list and click on the **Show Gallery** button. You will then see the images in that gallery as shown in this screenshot:

As you see, you can also create a new gallery by clicking on the **New Gallery** icon on the toolbar. This brings up a form as shown in the next screenshot. Just type the name of your new gallery and it's done! To upload any image to the gallery, click on the **Upload Picture** button.

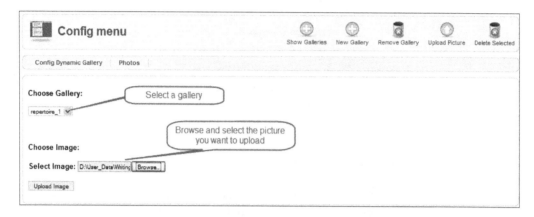

Depending on the number and size of the pictures and the speed of the internet connection, uploading the picture to your web server may take some time.

When accessed from the frontend, through a menu item, the photo gallery will look like the one shown in the following screenshot:

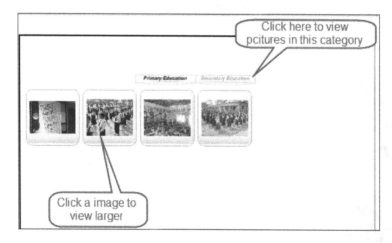

You can view the full image by clicking on its thumbnail. While viewing the full image, you can also apply the slideshow view.

Summary

There are many popular extensions for Joomla! that can show image galleries with Flash effects. In this chapter, we have learned about some of the popular and freely available extensions for building Flash image galleries in Joomla!. First, we have seen how to install, configure, and use the Expose gallery. Then, we moved on to another popular extension, Ozio Gallery. In the discussion of Ozio Gallery, we have seen that it can display images from a web server's directory as well as from a Flickr account. It has several skins with different effects. We have seen how to configure and use those skins with Ozio Gallery. Next, we moved on to the three simpler extensions: New Gallery, Simple Image Flash Gallery, and Dynamic Flash Gallery. We have seen how to configure and use these components in a Joomla! website.

In the next chapter we are going to learn about some more advanced Flash extensions and do some more exciting tasks, such as displaying maps, adding videos and mp3 players, adding a mindmap, adding streaming media, and showing the content in your desired fonts.

5

Flashier than Ever: Maps, Charts, Custom Fonts, Multimedia, and More

There are many possibilities of using Flash in a Joomla! website. We have explored some of these methods in the earlier chapters. We have seen how to embed Flash objects, Flash videos, and so on. In this chapter we will get familiar with some other uses of Flash on our Joomla!-based website. On completion of this chapter you will know how to:

- Use the YOS amMap extension to display interactive maps on your Joomla! website
- Use the YOS amChart component to display interactive graphical charts on your Joomla! website
- Use sIFR3 to display content on your site in any font even though the font is not installed on users' computers
- Use Flash based video players and build a streaming media site using the JVideo! extension for Joomla!
- Use Flash-based MP3 players on your site so that users can listen to music and other MP3 files online
- Visually represent your site's structure by creating a visual mind map using the Joom!FreeMind extension

To illustrate the use of extensions with Joomla! to serve a specific purpose, we have tried to cover those that are popular and freely available.

Showing maps using YOS amMap

Adding a map to your site may be a necessity in some cases. For example, you want to show the population of countries, or you want to show a world map to your students for teaching geography. Flash maps are always interesting as you can interact with them and can view them as you like. amMap provides tools for showing Flash maps. The amMap tool is ported as a Joomla! component by yOpensource, and the component is released with the name YOS amMap. This component has two versions—free and commercial. The commercial or pro version has some advanced features that are not available in the free version.

The YOS amMap component, together with its module, allows you to display a map of the world, a region, or a country. You can choose the map to be displayed, which areas or countries are to be highlighted, and the way in which the viewers can control the map. Generally, maps displayed through the YOS amMap component can be zoomed, centered, or scrolled to left, right, top, or bottom. You can also specify a color in which a region or a country should be displayed.

Installing and configuring YOS amMap

To use YOS amMap with your Joomla! website, you must first download it from `http://yopensource.com/en/component/remository/?func=fileinfo&id=3`. After downloading and extracting the compressed package, you get the component and module packages. Install the component and module from the **Extensions | Install/Uninstall** screen.

Once installed, you can administer the YOS amMap component from **Components | YOS amMap**. This shows the YOS amMap Control Panel, as shown in the following screenshot:

YOS amMap Control Panel displays several icons through which you can configure and publish maps. The first thing you should do is to configure the global settings for amMap. In order to do this, click on the **Parameters** icon in the toolbar. Doing so brings up the dialog box, as shown in the following screenshot:

In the **Global Configuration** section, you can enter a license key if you have purchased the commercial or the pro version of this component. For the free version, this is not needed. In this section, you can also configure the legal extensions of files that can be uploaded through this component, the maximum file size for uploads, the legal image extensions, and the allowed MIME types of all uploads. You can also specify whether the Flash uploader will be used or not. Once you have configured these fields, click on the **Save** button and return to **YOS amMap Control Panel**.

Adding map files

You can see the list of available maps by clicking on the **Maps** icon on the **YOS amMap Control Panel** screen or by clicking on **Components | amMap | Maps**. This shows the **Maps Manager** screen, as shown in the next screenshot.

As you can see, the **Maps Manager** screen displays the list of available maps. By default, you find the world.swf, continents.swf, and world_with_antartica.swf map files. You will find some extra maps with the amMap bundle. You can also download the original amMap package from http://www.ammap.com/download. After downloading the ZIP package, extract it, and you will find many maps in the maps subfolder. Any map from this folder can be uploaded to the Joomla! site from the **Maps Manager** screen.

Creating a map

There are several steps for creating a map using YOS amMap. First we need to upload the package for the map. For example, if we want to display the map of the United States of America, then we need to upload the map template, the map data file, and the map settings file for the United States of America. To do this first upload the map template from the **Maps Manager** screen. You will find the map template for USA in the **ammap/maps** folder. Then we need to upload the data and the settings files. For doing so, click on the **Upload** link on the **YOS amMap Control Panel** screen. Then, in the **Upload amMap** screen, which is shown in the next screenshot, type the map's title (**United States**) in the **Title** field. Before clicking on the **Browse** button besides the **Package File** field, you first add the ammap_data. xml and the ammap_settings.xml files to a single ZIP file, unitedstates.zip. Now, click on the **Browse** button, and select this unitedstates.zip file. Then click on the **Upload File & Install** button.

Once uploaded successfully, you see this map listed in the **YOS amMap Manager** screen, as shown in the next screenshot. You get this screen by clicking on the **amMaps** link on the toolbar.

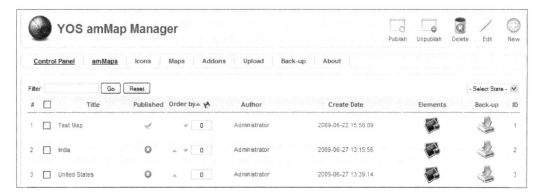

As you can see, the map that we have added is now listed in the **YOS amMap Manager** screen. However, the map is yet in an unpublished state, and we need to configure the map before publishing it. We need to configure its data and settings files, which are discussed in the following sections.

Map data file

The different regions of a map are identified by the map data file. This is an XML file and it defines the areas to be displayed on the map. The typical structure of a map data file can be understood by examining `ammap_data.xml`. The file has many comments that explain its structure. This file looks like as follows:

```xml
<?xml version="1.0" encoding="UTF-8"?>

<map map_file="maps/world.swf" tl_long="-168.49" tl_lat="83.63" br_
long="190.3" br_lat="-55.58" zoom_x="0%" zoom_y="0%" zoom="100%">
<areas>
    <area title="AFGHANISTAN" mc_name="AF"></area>
    <area title="ALAND ISLANDS" mc_name="AX"></area>
    <area title="BANGLADESH" mc_name="BD"></area>
    <area title="BHUTAN" mc_name="BT"></area>
    <area title="CANADA" mc_name="CA"></area>
    <area title="UNITED ARAB EMIRATES" mc_name="AE"></area>
    <area title="UNITED KINGDOM" mc_name="GB"></area>
    <area title="UNITED STATES" mc_name="US"></area>
    <area title="borders" mc_name="borders" color="#FFFFFF"
balloon="false"></area>
</areas>

<movies>
  <movie lat="51.3025" long="-0.0739" file="target" width="10"
  height="10" color="#CC0000" fixed_size="true" title="build-in
  movie usage example"></movie>

  <movie x="59.6667%" y="77.5%" file="icons/pin.swf" title="loaded
  movie usage example" text_box_width="250" text_box_height="140">
  <description>
    <![CDATA[You can add description text here. This text will
      appear the user clicks on the movie. this description text can
      be html-formatted (for a list which html tags are supported,
      visit <u>
<a href="http://livedocs.adobe.com/flash/8/main/00001459.html">this
  page</a></u>. You can add descriptions to areas and labels too.]]>
      </description>
    </movie>
</movies>
```

```
<labels>
    <label x="0" y="50" width="100%" align="center" text_size="16"
        color="#FFFFFF">
      <text><![CDATA[<b>World Map]]></text>
      <description><![CDATA[]]></description>
    </label>
</labels>
<lines>
    <line long="-0.0739, -74" lat="51.3025, 40.43" arrow="end"
        width="1" alpha="40"></line>
</lines>
</map>
```

This code is a stripped-down version of the default `ammap_data.xml` file. Let us examine its structure and try to understand the meaning of each markup:

- `<map> </map>`: You define the map's structure using this markup. First, by using the `map_file` attribute, we declare the map file that should be used to display this map. This markup has some other attributes through which we declare the top and the left offset in longitude and latitude. We can also specify the zooming level using the `zoom_x`, `zoom_y`, and `zoom` attributes.

- `<areas> </areas>`: Areas are the regions or countries on a map. These are defined in the map. We only need to define the areas that we want to display. For example, in the sample, we have defined eight countries to be displayed and one straight line. Each area element has several attributes, among which you need to mention `mc_name` and `title`. You specify the area's name in `mc_name`, which is predefined in the map template. The title element will be displayed as the title of that map area. For example, `<area mc_name="BD" title="Bangladesh"></area>` means the areas marked as `BD` in the map template will be displayed with the title `Bangladesh`. In order to specify the `mc_name` element, you need to follow the map template designer's instructions.

- `<movies> </movies>`: Movies are some extra clips that can be displayed as a separate layer on the map. For example, to display the capital of each country, a movie clip could be displayed in the specified latitude and longitude. You can also display some other animations or text using a movie definition.

- `<labels> </labels>`: The `<labels>` markup contains the text to be displayed on the map. You can add any text on a map by defining a label element.

To view and edit the map data file, `ammap_data.xml`, click on the map name on the **YOS amMap Manager** screen. This opens-up the **amMap: [Edit]** screen, as shown in the following screenshot:

The **amMap: [Edit]** screen displays several configurations for the map. From the **Details** section you can change the map name, publish the map, and enable security. From the **Design** section you can view and edit the data and the settings files. Clicking on **Data** will show the data file. You can edit the data file from the online editor. As we want to display the map of USA, we will make the following changes on this screen:

1. Select `usa.swf` in the **Maps** list.

2. Change the data file as follows:

```
<?xml version="1.0" encoding="UTF-8"?>
<map map_file="maps/usa.swf" zoom="100%" zoom_x="7.8%"
    zoom_y="0.18%">

<areas>
 <area mc_name="AL" title="Alabama"/>
 <area mc_name="AK" title="Alaska"/>
```

```
<area mc_name="AZ" title="Arizona"/>
<area mc_name="AR" title="Arkansas"/>
<area mc_name="CA" title="California"/>
<area mc_name="CO" title="Colorado"/>
<area mc_name="CT" title="Connecticut"/>
<area mc_name="DE" title="Delaware"/>
<area mc_name="DC" title="District of Columbia"/>
<area mc_name="FL" title="Florida"/>
<area mc_name="GA" title="Georgia"/>
<area mc_name="HI" title="Hawaii"/>
<area mc_name="ID" title="Idaho"/>
<area mc_name="IL" title="Illinois"/>
<area mc_name="IN" title="Indiana"/>
<area mc_name="IA" title="Iowa"/>
<area mc_name="KS" title="Kansas"/>
<area mc_name="KY" title="Kentucky"/>
<area mc_name="LA" title="Louisiana"/>
<area mc_name="ME" title="Maine"/>
<area mc_name="MD" title="Maryland"/>
<area mc_name="MA" title="Massachusetts"/>
<area mc_name="MI" title="Michigan"/>
<area mc_name="MN" title="Minnesota"/>
<area mc_name="MS" title="Mississippi"/>
<area mc_name="MO" title="Missouri"/>
<area mc_name="MT" title="Montana"/>
<area mc_name="NE" title="Nebraska"/>
<area mc_name="NV" title="Nevada"/>
<area mc_name="NH" title="New Hampshire"/>
<area mc_name="NJ" title="New Jersey"/>
<area mc_name="NM" title="New Mexico"/>
<area mc_name="NY" title="New York"/>
<area mc_name="NC" title="North Carolina"/>
<area mc_name="ND" title="North Dakota"/>
<area mc_name="OH" title="Ohio"/>
<area mc_name="OK" title="Oklahoma"/>
<area mc_name="OR" title="Oregon"/>
<area mc_name="PA" title="Pennsylvania"/>
<area mc_name="RI" title="Rhode Island"/>
<area mc_name="SC" title="South Carolina"/>
<area mc_name="SD" title="South Dakota"/>
<area mc_name="TN" title="Tennessee"/>
```

```
<area mc_name="TX" title="Texas"/>
<area mc_name="UT" title="Utah"/>
<area mc_name="VT" title="Vermont"/>
<area mc_name="VA" title="Virginia"/>
<area mc_name="WA" title="Washington"/>
<area mc_name="WV" title="West Virginia"/>
<area mc_name="WI" title="Wisconsin"/>
<area mc_name="WY" title="Wyoming"/>
</areas>
<labels>
  <label x="0" y="60" width="100%" color="#FFFFFF"        text_
size="18">
    <text>Map of the United States of America</text>
  </label>
</labels>
</map>
```

As you can see, we have defined regions (states) on the map of USA,
and towards the end of the file, we have added a label for the map.

3. Select **Yes** for the **Published** field in the **Details** section.

When you are done making these changes click on the **Save** button to save these
changes. Now we will look into the map settings file.

> Map data files for countries are available with the amMap package. Thus,
> if you download amMap 2.5.1, you will get the map settings files for
> different countries. For example, the map data file for USA will be in the
> amMap_2.5.1/examples/_countries/usa folder.

Map settings file

The map settings file is another XML file through which the map's display and other
settings are defined. You can view and edit this file in the same way as you have
done for the map data file, ammap_data.xml. A map settings file is named as
ammap_settings.xml, and like the ammap_data.xml file, it has lots of annotations to
explain each setting. You can view as well as edit this file by clicking on the **Settings**
section in the **amMap: [Edit]** screen, as shown in the following screenshot:

An annotation for each setting is provided on the right side. You can configure the settings by following the instructions in the annotations. Once the changes have been made to this file, click on the **Save** icon on the toolbar to save the changes and close the screen.

Publishing a map through the module

After configuring the map through the **amMap: [Edit]** screen and editing the map data file, `ammap_data.xml` and the map settings file, `ammap_settings.xml`, you can display the map on the frontend by publishing the amMap module.

If you have not installed the amMap module yet, then install it from the **Extensions | Install/Uninstall** screen. The module and the plugin installation packages are bundled with the YOS amMap package that you have already downloaded. Once installed, go to **Extensions | Module Manager** and click on the **YOS amMap** module. That shows the **Module: [Edit]** screen for the YOS amMap module, as shown in the following screenshot:

Like other modules you can use the **Details** section to provide a title for this module, publish the module, select the position where it should be displayed, set the access level, and establish the order of display. Similarly, from the **Menu Assignment** section, you can specify the menus for which the module will be displayed. The settings specific to this module are displayed in the **Parameters** section. First you need to type the **amMap's ID**, which is displayed in the list shown on the **YOS amMap Manager** screen. After typing the **amMap's ID**, select **Yes** in the **Enable Plugin** field if you want to show this map using a plugin.

The next few settings are for displaying the map in your desired format. You can assign a module suffix (for example, green), which can be used to manipulate the display through a CSS. In the **Display-Type** drop-down box, select either **SWF-Object** or **Embedding Flash Object**. **SWF-Object** is the default mode and it uses a wrapper for embedding Flash objects. Then you can specify the width and height of the Flash object in pixels. This needs to be in line with your module's position. You can also specify the version of Flash needed to display the map. The default value for this field is **8**, which means that Flash Player version 8 will display the map properly, and users having a version lower than this will be prompted to upgrade to the required version of Flash Player. In the **Background Color** field you can specify the background color for the module.

The path to the amMap files can be specified in the **Path** field. The default value for this field is `components/com_yos_ammap/ammap`, which is fine as the files are installed in this directory. You can specify default data and settings files in the **Data file** and **Setting file** fields. The default values for these fields are `components/com_yos_ammap/ammap/ammap_data.xml` and `components/com_yos_ammap/ammap/ammap_settings.xml` respectively. The files specified in these two fields will work only when no ID number for amMap is specified in the **amMap's ID** field.

You can specify a preloader color, a loading text, and a settings loading text. These texts are displayed when the map's data and settings are being loaded.

When all these settings have been set and saved by clicking on the **Save** button on the toolbar, you can preview the map by clicking on the **Preview** button on the toolbar. The map should be displayed as shown in the following screenshot, in the frontend:

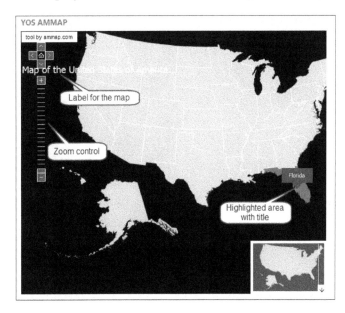

When you move your mouse pointer over the map area you will see that the states are highlighted displaying the state's name. You can zoom in or zoom out using the Zoom control shown on the left of the map. Note that an overview map is displayed at the bottom-right corner. Clicking the arrow below it will hide the overview map.

If you want to display multiple maps, then you can copy the **YOS amMap** module and configure each instance with a different amMap ID. To copy the module, in the **Extensions | Module Manager** screen, select the module and click on the **Copy** icon in the toolbar. Then, rename the copied module. Alternatively, you can use the new module wizard by clicking on the **New** icon on the toolbar. In this wizard, you have to select **YOS amMap** in the **Module: [New]** screen and then configure it with the same settings, as described above.

Showing the map in content using a plugin

So far we have seen how to display a Flash map with the amMap module. You can also display the map in your Joomla! content, that is, articles. The YOS amMap component package comes with a plugin for displaying an amMap map into Joomla! articles. If you have installed the plugin already, then go to **Extensions | Plugin Manager** and click on **Plugin - YOS Ammap**. This displays the **Plugin: [Edit]** screen, shown in the following screenshot, for the **YOS Ammap** plugin:

Enable this plugin by selecting **Yes** in the **Enabled** field. Next, read the instructions given in the **Description** field. The instructions show how to use this plugin. From this text, you will notice that you can embed an amMap map in articles using the following syntax:

```
{yos_ammap mapid='3' width='500' height='400' flashv='8'
bgcolour='#000000' type='js' plugin='1'}
```

You may be familiar with most of these by now. First, we have to specify the `mapid`, and then its width, height, flash version, background color, type, and plugin. Use `1` in `plugin` if you want to show dynamic data in the map. Therefore, using this syntax, we can add the map of USA in an article. The text for the article may be as follows:

```
amMap is an interactive flash map creation software. Use this tool to
show locations of your offices, routes of your journeys, create your
distributor map. Photos or illustrations can be used instead of maps,
so you can make different presentations, e-learning tools and more.
YOS amMap is an Joomla extension which integrated almost amMap
features. With YOS amMap you can easily integrate maps which provided
by amMap to your Joomla site.
You can also include a map in Joomla! artilcle. Here is an example:

{yos_ammap mapid='3' width='600' height='500' falshv='8' plugin='1'}
```

The last line, inside { }, will show the map with the ID 3, which is the map of USA. When this article is published and viewed in the frontend, the article will look like the following screenshot:

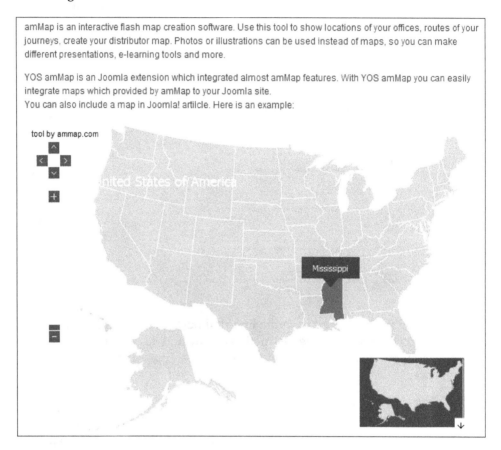

As you see, the map of USA has been embedded in the article. The map behaves in the same way as it does inside the module. You can add multiple maps in an article using the same syntax. However, you must ensure that the map IDs are correct.

 For more information on using the YOS amMap component, please visit `http://yopensource.com/en/documentation/yos-ammap`. You can also check `www.ammap.com` for more information on amMap and to download new map files.

Showing charts using YOS amChart

Like maps, you can also display interactive Flash charts on your Joomla! website. The YOS amChart component, from `http://www.yopensource.com`, allows you to add several types of charts on your Joomla! website. Like YOS amMap, this component is also available in two versions: free and pro. You can download the free version from `http://www.yopensource.com/en/download?func=fileinfo&id=4`. Unzip the package once you have downloaded it. You will find three files: one for component, one for module, and one for plugin. Install these three files from the **Extensions | Install/Uninstall** screen.

Configuring YOS amChart

Once you have installed the component, you can configure it from the **Components | YOS amChart | Control Panel. YOS amChart Control Panel** screen, which looks like the following screenshot:

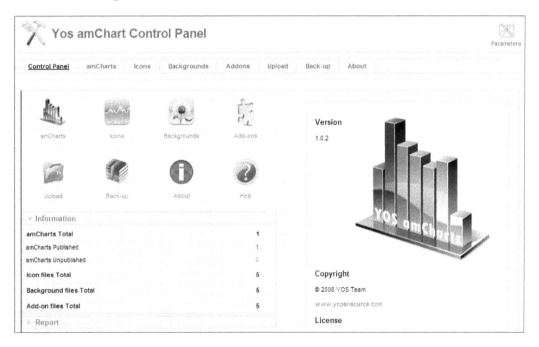

As you can see, the **YOS amChart Control Panel** is similar to the **YOS amMap Control Panel**. From here you can view information about charts, icons, background files, and add-on files. As with the YOS amMap component, you can set the global configurations for this component by clicking on the **Parameters** icon on the top-right corner.

Creating a chart

Before you can use a chart on your Joomla! website, you need to create the chart first. For creating the chart, click on the **amCharts** link on the toolbar. This shows the **YOS amChart Manager** screen, as shown in the following screenshot:

The **YOS amCharts Manager** screen will list the charts that have already been made. To create a new chart click on the **New** icon on the toolbar. This opens the **amChart: [New]** screen, as shown in the following screenshot:

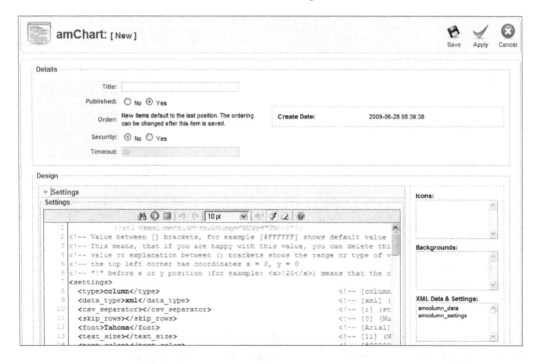

Type a title for the chart in the **Title** field. Then select **Yes** in the **Published** field. If your data is sensitive, then select **Yes** in the **Security** field, and then specify a timeout value in minutes.

In the **Design** section you can edit the settings and the data files. First, click on **Settings** to view and edit the `amcolumn_settings.xml` file. Then, edit the `amcolumn_data.xml` file. The structure of these two files is described in the following sections.

amChart settings file

By default, you will find the `amcolumn_settings.xml` file as the settings file. You can view and edit this file by clicking on **Settings** in the **Design** section of the **amChart: [New]** screen. The file starts with an XML declaration and then continues with the `<settings>` markup. Under the `<settings>` element we find the following block:

```
<settings>
    <type>column</type>
    <data_type>xml</data_type>
    <csv_separator></csv_separator>
    <skip_rows></skip_rows>
    <font>Tahoma</font>
    <text_size></text_size>
    <text_color></text_color>
    <decimals_separator></decimals_separator>
    <thousands_separator></thousands_separator>
    <digits_after_decimal></digits_after_decimal>
    <redraw></redraw>
    <reload_data_interval></reload_data_interval>
    <preloader_on_reload></preloader_on_reload>
    <add_time_stamp></add_time_stamp>
    <precision></precision>
    <depth>0</depth>
    <angle>0</angle>
    <colors></colors>
```

For all of the above declarations, annotations are present to the right. The annotations explain the purpose of each declaration, their possible values, and the default value (inside the square brackets []). As we want to make a column chart, we will use `<type>column</type>` in our settings file.

Note that you can use two types of data files: an XML file or a CSV file. Although making a CSV data file is easier, it is better to use an XML data file as we can specify many attributes in an XML data file, which is not possible in a CSV data file. Some of the declarations in the code block shown at the starting of this section are specific to a CSV data file, and you only need these settings when using a CSV data file.

When we are using a column chart, we can define the structure of the column in the `<column>` declaration as follows:

```
<column>
    <type>Clustered</type>
    <width>85</width>
    <spacing>4</spacing>
    <grow_time>3</grow_time>
    <grow_effect>strong</grow_effect>
    <sequenced_grow>true</sequenced_grow>
    <alpha></alpha>
    <border_color></border_color>
    <border_alpha></border_alpha>
    <data_labels>
        <![CDATA[{series}:{value}]]>
    </data_labels>
    <data_labels_text_color></data_labels_text_color>
    <data_labels_text_size>12</data_labels_text_size>
    <data_labels_position>above</data_labels_position>
    <balloon_text>
      <![CDATA[Number of Schools - {series} : {value}]]>
    </balloon_text>
    <link_target></link_target>
    <gradient></gradient>
    <bullet_offset></bullet_offset>
    <hover_brightness>30</hover_brightness>
</column>
```

Like all other codes, this code block also has annotations and possible values for each element.

After defining the column settings, we may also define a category and value axes, a balloon, and a legend. We also need to configure the labels as follows:

```
<labels>
  <label lid="0">
        <x>10</x>
        <y>400</y>
    <rotate>true</rotate>
    <width></width>
    <align>center</align>
    <text_color></text_color>
    <text_size>14</text_size>
    <text>
    <![CDATA[<b>Number of primary Schools (1970 - 2005)</b>]]>
```

```
        </text>
    </label>
    <label lid="1">
        <x>0</x>
        <y>380</y>
        <width></width>
        <align>right</align>
        <text_color></text_color>
        <text_size>14</text_size>
        <text>
          <![CDATA[Source: <a href="http://banbeis.gov.bd/
            trend_analysis1.htm" target="_blank"><u>Bangladesh Bureau
            of Educational Information and Statistics</u></a>]]>
        </text>
    </label>
    </labels>
```

This code will add two labels: one for the y-axis and another as text for the data source. Finally, we define the settings for the graphs as follows:

```
    <graphs>
      <graph gid="1">
<type>column</type>
        <title>Growth of Primary Schools (1970 - 2005)</title>
        <color>B92F2F</color>
<alpha></alpha>
<data_labels>
        <![CDATA[{series}: {value}]]>
</data_labels>
        <gradient_fill_colors></gradient_fill_colors>
        <balloon_color></balloon_color>
        <balloon_alpha></balloon_alpha>
        <balloon_text_color></balloon_text_color>
          <balloon_text>
          <![CDATA[Number of primary schools- {series}: {value}]]>
        </balloon_text>
        <fill_alpha></fill_alpha>
        <width></width>
      <bullet></bullet>
        <bullet_size></bullet_size>
        <bullet_color></bullet_color>
        <visible_in_legend></visible_in_legend>

    </graphs>
```

The settings for graphs can also be in a data file. The previous code block shows the settings for a single column graph. You must ensure that the `gid` mentioned here matches the `gid` mentioned in the data file. Now we will examine the `amcolumn_data.xml` file.

amChart data file

The default XML data file can be viewed and edited by clicking on **Data** in the **Design** section of the **amChart: [New]** screen. The structure of the data file is simple, as shown here:

```
<?xml version="1.0" encoding="UTF-8"?>
<chart>
    <series>
        <value xid="100">1950</value>
        <value xid="101">1951</value>
        <value xid="102">1952</value>
    </series>
     <graphs>
        <graph gid="1">
            <value xid="100" color="#318DBD">-0.307</value>
            <value xid="101" color="#318DBD">-0.168</value>
            <value xid="102" color="#318DBD">-0.073</value>
        </graph>
     </graphs>
</chart>
```

We want to display data, as shown in the following table:

Year	Number of Schools
1970	29082
1975	39914
1980	43936
1985	44220
1990	47241
1995	62654
2000	76809
2005	80397

We can represent the above data in an XML data file as follows:

```xml
<?xml version="1.0" encoding="UTF-8"?>
<chart>
    <series>
        <value xid="1">1970</value>
        <value xid="2">1975</value>
        <value xid="3">1980</value>
        <value xid="4">1985</value>
        <value xid="5">1990</value>
        <value xid="6">1995</value>
        <value xid="7">2000</value>
        <value xid="8">2005</value>
    </series>
    <graphs>
        <graph gid="1">
            <value xid="1" color="#e5684f">29082</value>
            <value xid="2" color="#e5a783">39914</value>
            <value xid="3" color="#e5b266">43936</value>
            <value xid="4" color="#375ce5">44220</value>
            <value xid="5" color="#8c92e5">47241</value>
            <value xid="6" color="#a0a4e5">62654</value>
            <value xid="7" color="#5be516">76809</value>
            <value xid="8" color="#3e9c0f">80397</value>
        </graph>
    </graphs>
</chart>
```

To specify hexadecimal code for the colors of each column, you can use **Color Picker** from the right side of the editing screen. When you are done with editing this file, click on the **Save** icon on the toolbar. When you have saved the data, you see the chart listed in the **YOS amChart Manager** screen, as shown in the following screenshot:

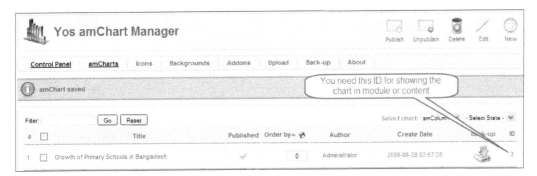

Note the **ID** for the chart you have created. You need this ID to display the chart through the amChart module or plugin.

Publishing the chart through the module

Once you have created an amChart you can publish it to your site through the YOS amChart module. If you have not installed the module yet, then install it from **Extensions | Install/Uninstall** and then go to **Extensions | Module Manager**. From the list of modules, click on the **YOS amChart** module. That opens the **Module: [Edit]** screen for the **YOS amChart** module. Like other modules, select **Yes** in the **Published** field, a position to display the module, and an order from the **Details** section. The module-specific settings are in the **Parameters** section, as shown in the following screenshot:

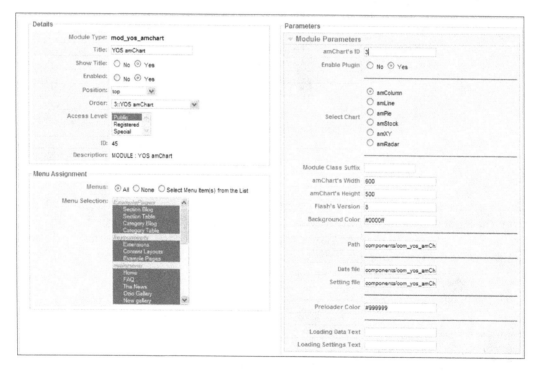

In the **amChart's ID** field, type the ID for the chart you want to display. For the chart that we created earlier, the ID is 3. Therefore, we type **3** in this field. Select **Yes** in the **Enable Plugin** field so that you can embed this chart using the YOS amChart plugin. From the **Select Chart** field, select the type of chart you want to display. Select **amColumn** as we want to display a column chart. The rest of the settings are similar to the **amMap** module settings. You can specify the width and height of the chart, a background color, the path of amChart files, the default path to the data and settings files, the preloader color, the loading text, and the loading settings text. Finally click on the **Save** icon on the toolbar to save the settings for this module. Now on previewing the site from the frontend you find the module with the chart displayed, as shown in the following screenshot:

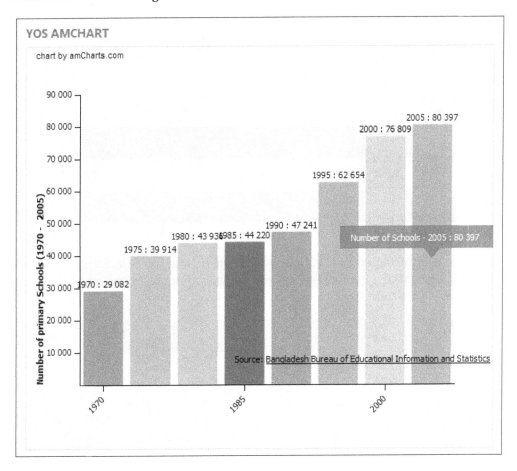

Changing the value of the **Select Chart** field in the module configuration screen has no effect, unless you define the same in chart settings. For example, we have defined a chart of a column type. If you select the chart type as pie in the module settings, the chart will still display as a column chart as it is defined as such in the graph settings XML file. Therefore, always use the same type as specified in the XML file definition.

So far we have seen how to create a column chart using the amChart component. We can also create other types of charts such as line charts, pie charts, stock charts, XY charts, and radar charts. For each type of chart, structure of the data file and the settings file is separate. Now we will learn how to create a pie chart.

You can create any type of chart from the **YOS amChart Manager** screen:

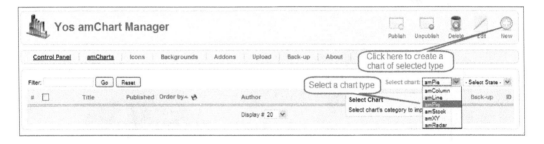

The trick is to select the chart type you need from the **Select chart** drop-down list and then clicking the **New** icon on the toolbar to create a chart of the selected type

As we want to create a new pie chart, we select **amPie** from the **Select chart** drop-down list. Clicking on the **New** icon on the toolbar opens up the **amChart: [New]** screen shown in the following screenshot:

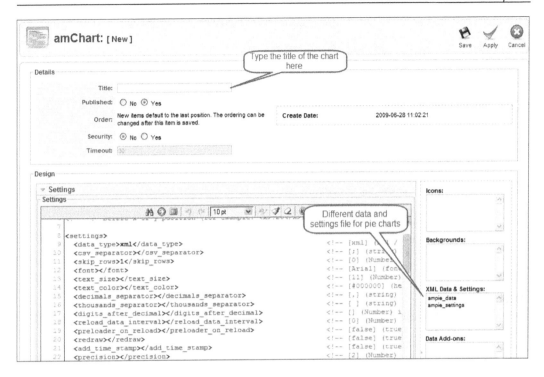

Note that the **amChart: [New]** screen is similar to that for creating
a column chart. The only difference is that it has separate XML data and settings
files—ampie_data.xml and ampie_settings.xml. In most cases, you do not need to
edit the ampie_settings.xml file, except for changing the labels. But to reflect your
data you need to modify the ampie_data.xml file. Consider that we want to display
the following data in a pie chart, for example:

Type of Primary School	Number of School
Government Primary School	37672
Registered Non-Govt. Primary School	19682
Non-Registered Non-Govt. Primary School	946
Other Primary Level Institution	22097

This data can be represented in the `ampie_data.xml` file as follows:

```xml
<?xml version="1.0" encoding="UTF-8"?>
<pie>

   <slice title="Government Primary School" color="#5be516"> 37672
   </slice>
   <slice title="Registered Non-Govt. Primary School"
         color="#e545b8">19682
   </slice>
   <slice title="Non-Registered Non-Govt. Primary School"
         color="#56a1d6">946
   </slice>
   <slice title="Other Primary Level Institution"
         color="#f3f85b">22097
   </slice>
</pie>
```

After changing the data file, click on the **Save** icon on the toolbar. Then using **Extensions | Module Manager**, copy the YOS amChart module and rename it as YOS amChart Pie. Change the **Settings** as shown in the following screenshot:

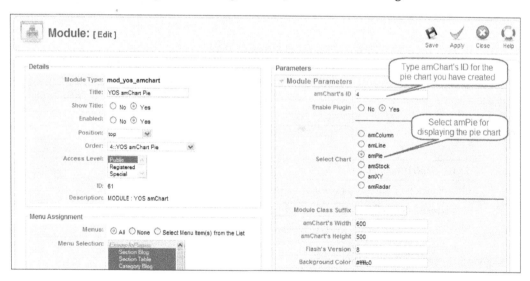

Once you've published the module, preview the frontend, and you will see the module with the pie chart you have created. The pie chart will look like the one shown in the following screenshot:

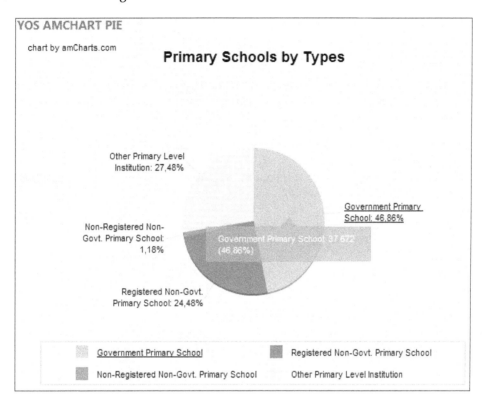

As you can see, the pie chart is displayed with the legends and data labels. The slices are displayed in the color we have specified. Taking the mouse pointer on a legend item will highlight the corresponding slice in the pie and display its label and data.

The pie chart shown in the previous screenshot is simple and without 3D effects. We can add 3D effects and pull one or two slices out. To do this, add the following lines of code in the `ampie_settings.xml` file:

```
<pie>
    <x></x>
    <y></y>
    <radius>90</radius>
    <inner_radius></inner_radius>
    <height>10</height>
    <angle>45</angle>
    <outline_color>0xFF0F00</outline_color>
```

```
    <outline_alpha>10</outline_alpha>
<base_color></base_color>
<brightness_step></brightness_step>
<colors></colors>
<link_target></link_target>
<alpha></alpha>
<pie>
```

The highlighted lines in this code block are for adding a 3D effect to the pie chart. If we want to make one slice appear pulled out, then we can add that in the XML data file as follows:

```
<slice title="Government Primary School" color="#5be516">37672
</slice>
<slice title="Registered Non-Govt. Primary School" color="#e545b8"
       pull_out="true">19682
</slice>
<slice title="Non-Registered Non-Govt. Primary School"
       color="#56a1d6" pull_out="true">946
</slice>
<slice title="Other Primary Level Institution" color="#f3f85b">22097
</slice>
```

In the two highlighted lines of this code we have added `pull_out="true"` to pull these slices out in the pie chart. When the changes are saved and the module is previewed, the pie chart will appear as shown in the following screenshot:

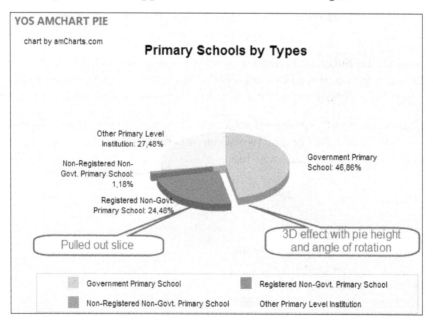

As you see, the pie chart now looks like a 3D pie chart. The slices marked for pull out are also displayed now as if they were pulled out from the pie.

Embedding the chart in content using a plugin

Like amMap, you can embed charts into Joomla! articles using the YOS amChart plugin. If you have not installed the plugin yet, then install it, and go to **Extensions | Plugin Manager**. Then click on the **Plugin – YOS Amchart** plugin, which brings up the **Plugin: [Edit]** screen, as shown in the following screenshot:

In the **Plugin: [Edit]** screen, select **Yes** in the **Enabled** field and set the **Access Level** and **Order**. In the **Description** field, you get the instructions on using this plugin. Once this plugin is enabled, amChart can be embedded into any Joomla! content using the following syntax:

```
{yos_amchart chartid='4' width='500' height='500' flashv='8'
   bgcolour='#ffffc0' plugin='1'}
```

As you can see, the syntax is similar to that of the amMap plugin. Here you specify the chart ID, width, height, Flash version number, background color, and enable/disable use of dynamic data. The above line in an article will display the chart, as shown in the following screenshot:

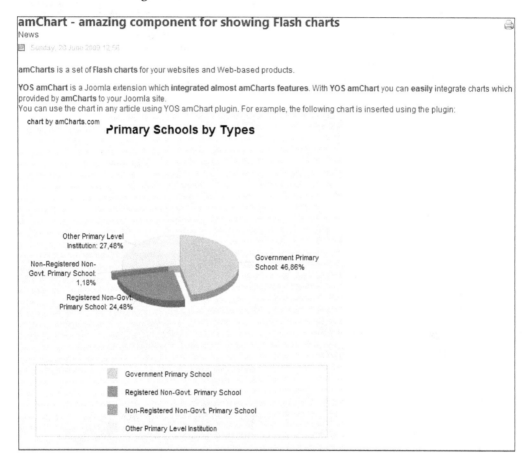

As you can see, the chart with the specified chart ID is displayed in the place where we have used the {yos_amchart ... } markup. Multiple charts can also be embedded in an article using separate {yos_amchart } markups.

Showing the content in any font using sIFR

If you have ever designed a website, then you know how frustrating it is to decide on the fonts to be used. The font you use for the text on your website will be rendered properly only when the users have the same font installed on their computers. As an alternative some designers try to use images with fancy fonts, and some also like using Flash. However, replacing text with an image or Flash is a big compromise as these are not indexed by search engines. It also hampers accessibility. To solve this problem of typography on the Web, a Flash-based technique known as **Scalable Inman Flash Replacement (sIFR)** is used. sIFR works as follows:

1. You identify the text to be replaced with sIFR.

2. A JavaScript runs to check whether Flash is installed on the user's computer. It then checks the markups that you have used to enable sIFR.

3. If Flash is not installed or JavaScript is not enabled, then the web page is rendered in plain HTML as per your markup. If Flash is installed, then JavaScript traverses through your page to find out the elements marked for using sIFR.

4. Once the elements to be rendered using sIFR have been identified, Flash animations are created taking the texts as parameters.

5. The ActionScript inside each Flash animation then draws the text in the designated typefaces. It also scales up to fit the Flash animation.

All of this searching, replacing, and rendering happens in a second. As a result, the user can see the text rendered as it was intended to be.

You can use the sIFR technique with your Joomla! website. There are several plugins for rendering the text of a Joomla! website through sIFR. One such freely available plugin is JsIFR3, available at `http://club.freakedout.de/jsifr3-and-jsifr3-pro.html`. Once downloaded and installed, you can see it listed in the **Extensions | Plugin Manager** screen. Click on **System - JsIFR3**, and that shows the **Plugin: [Edit]** screen, as shown in the following screenshot:

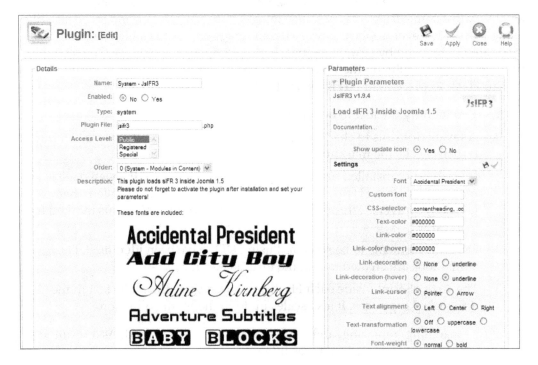

Enable the plugin from the **Details** section by selecting **Yes** in the **Enabled** field and read the instructions provided in the **Description** field. Samples of the fonts are also displayed in this field. On the right, you see the plugin-specific settings in the **Plugin Parameters** section. In the **Settings** area, first select the font from the **Font** drop-down list. The text elements marked to be displayed using sIFR will be rendered in the font selected here. If you want to use some other font not listed in the **Font** drop-down list, then type the name in the **Custom font** field. For example, if you have a file called `arial.swf`, then you need to type 'Arial' in this field to use that font. The `arial.swf` file also has to be uploaded to the `/plugins/system/jsifr3` folder.

In the **CSS-selector** field, there is a list of CSS selectors with which the text will be rendered using sIFR. By default, you see a list comprising of **.contentheading**, **.componentheading**, **.contentpagetitle**, **h1**, **h2**, **h3**, **h4**, **h5**, **h6**. You can edit this list and add your desired CSS selector here. The next few fields are for specifying the text color, link color, link decoration, link cursor, text alignment, text transformation, font weight, font style, letter spacing, margin, and offset from left, right, top, and bottom. It is always good to select **On** in the **Exact size** field as that prevents the text from overlapping. However, you can force all of the text in one line by selecting **On** in the **Single line** field.

From the **Dropshadow** section, you can set how the dropshadow effect should be used. You can specify the color, the distance from the text, the strength of the dropshadow, the alpha value for the dropshadow, the blur effect from the right and bottom, and if inner/outer shadow is to be used.

When these fields are configured, click on the **Save** icon on the toolbar to save the settings. Now the plugin is active and the elements with specified CSS selectors will be displayed in the font we have selected in this configuration. With this configuration the web page will look as shown in the following screenshot:

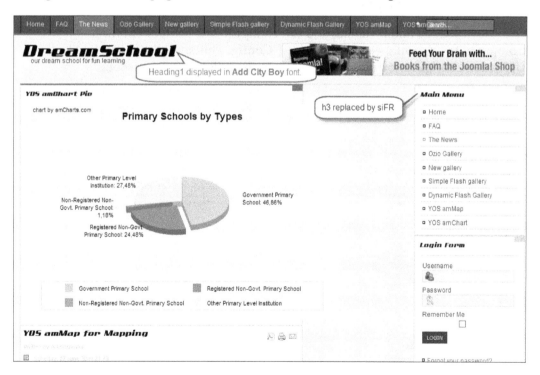

As you can see, the headings through h1 to h4 are replaced by the sIFR designated fonts. If you right-click on the element, then you find that a Flash object is present. However, view the source for the page, and you still find an equivalent text for the Flash object.

By default, 11 fonts are bundled with the JsIFR3 free version package. However, you can use only one font at a time. To overcome this, you may use the JsIFR3 pro version, which supports the use of five different styles at one time.

Using Flash uploader

Flash uploaders provide some convenience over the normal HTML upload methods. With a Flash uploader, we can upload multiple files at a time, view the file hierarchy, and so on. There are several components and plugins for using Flash uploaders with Joomla!. One such component is **Joomla! Flash Uploader** (Joomla! 1.5) or in short **JFU** and is freely available at `http://www.tinywebgallery.com/dl.php?file=jfu_291_J15`.

Once downloaded and installed, you can configure this component from **Components | Joomla! Flash Uploader | Config**. This shows the **Joomla! Flash Uploader Configuration** screen, as shown in the following screenshot:

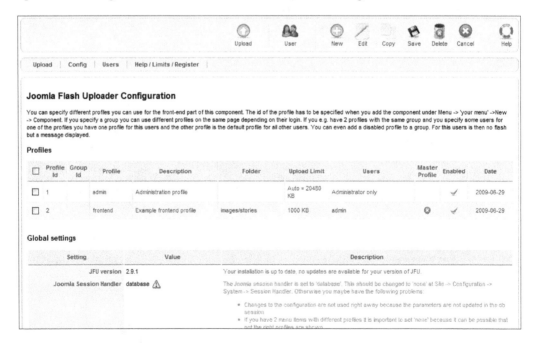

As you can see, different profiles can be created for JFU. For example, you can create a profile for administrators, who may have the highest privilege in uploading files. On the other hand, for frontend users, a separate profile can be created with limited upload privilege. You can create a new profile by clicking on the **New** icon on the toolbar. Doing so brings up the Joomla Flash Uploader profile creation form, as shown in the following screenshot:

While defining a profile, you can configure several privileges for uploading files in Joomla!. Click on the **Users** link to assign the registered users to each profile, as shown in the following screenshot:

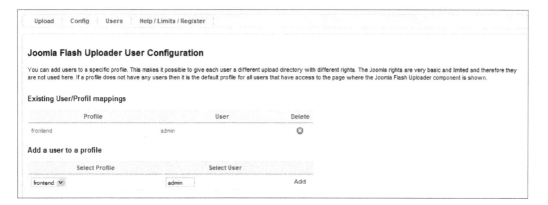

When you have created an appropriate profile and assigned users to it, the Flash uploader can be used from the frontend too. To try this uploader instantly, click on the **Upload** link. This shows the Joomla! Flash Uploader, as shown in the following screenshot:

You can see the list of folders and files available on the web server in this screen. Once you select a folder or a file, you can delete it by clicking on the **Delete** button. By clicking on the **Options** button, you can select to create a new folder, rename a selected folder or file, or delete a folder or a file. To upload new files, click on the **Add files** button, browse to the appropriate folder on your hard disk, and select files to upload. The added files will be displayed in the queue. Once this is done, click on the **Upload** button to upload the files to the web server. A progress bar will be displayed to inform you about the status of the upload.

To use the Flash uploader in the frontend, you can create a menu item for Joomla! Flash Uploader. Another way of displaying the Flash uploader is by using the plugin. Indeed, with the Joomla! Flash Uploader plugin, you can add the uploader to any Joomla! article. You can find out more about the Joomla! Flash Uploader plugin and download it from `http://www.tinywebgallery.com/en/tfu/web_jfu.php`. Once downloaded and installed, enable the plugin using **Extensions | Plugin Manager**.

Using this plugin is simple. You can add the Flash uploader to any content by using the following line of code:

```
{joomla_flash_uploader type=<0 or 1> id=<profile or group id>}
```

Here, the value of `type` can be either `0` or `1`. A value of `0` means *profile* and `1` means *group*. In the `id` attribute, you need to type either the profile ID or the group ID based on the `type` setting. Thus, if we want to use a Flash uploader that will use profile number 2 (frontend), for example, then in an article, we simply put the following line of code:

```
{joomla_flash_uploader type=0 id=2}
```

The Flash uploader will then be displayed in the article, as shown in the following screenshot:

Joomla Flash Uploader

News

▦ Monday, 29 June 2009 22:52

The Joomla Flash Uploader is the Joomla component of the TWG Flash Uploader.

You now have the possibility to upload files to your web server the easiest way possible. You simply select the files you war HTML form anymore where you have to upload each file individually. You only need Flash 8 or higher installed to use this co

You can upload files in the backend of Joomla AND you can offer this in the front-end for your users as well. You can create your joomla users. This gives you the possibility to give e.g. every of your users a different upload directory and/or different ri

Uploading was never easier!

here is the uploader:

Joomla Flash Uploader - Upload folder: ./images/stories/borhan			🌐

Remote	0 files (0k)	Upload Queue	Upload size: 0 KB
Name		Name	Size	Date

Delete				
Refresh		Add files	Remove	**Resize** Original ▾ Upload

Status: Please select your files to upload. Upload maximum file size (per file): 1000 KB. [?]

One of the good features of using such a plugin is that it can be configured to upload files to the user's sub-directory. The profile used in our example is configured to upload to a sub-directory created after the login name of the user. In this case, when the user logs in to Joomla! and uploads the files, the files are stored in the user's own directory, for example /images/stories/borhan, where borhan is the login name of the user.

Creating a streaming media site

There are several Flash-based video players that can be used on a Joomla! site. We have already seen two such video players in Chapter 2, *Enhance Your Joomla! Content with Flash*. Now, we will look at some other Flash-based video players that can be used in a Joomla! website for displaying Flash movies and for creating a streaming media site.

Installing and configuring JVideo!

JVideo! is a component for displaying videos on your Joomla! site. It has two versions: free and professional. The professional version allows branding of the player and some other features that are not in the free version. For both professional and free versions, you need to create an account at www.infinovision.com. Each time you use the dashboard for JVideo!, this login information will be required. To find out more about JVideo! and to download it, visit http://jvideo.infinovision.com/.

Once downloaded and installed, you can configure this component using **Extensions | JVideo!**. This will show the **JVideo!** Screen, as shown in the following screenshot:

As you can see, the **JVideo!** screen displays several icons. Click on one of these to configure and manage the video repository. First, we need to set the global configurations for this component. Click on **Configuration** to get the **Global Configuration** screen, as shown in the following screenshot:

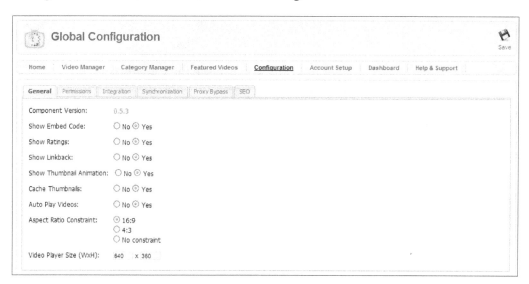

The **Global Configuration** screen has six tabs: **General**, **Permissions**, **Integration**, **Synchronization**, **Proxy Bypass**, and **SEO**. From the **General** tab, you can enable showing the embed code, the ratings, the thumbnail animation, and also enable auto playing of videos. You can also set the aspect ratio size of the video player.

From the **Permissions** tab, you set what will be the minimum group membership requirement for uploading videos, whether uploaded videos need approval, and if so, then which of the groups can approve the uploaded videos. You can also specify the maximum upload size, the maximum duration, and the maximum number of videos a user can upload.

From the **Integration** tab, you can define the video system, comments system, and profile system to be used for JVideo!. By default, we can use only one video system, **Infinovision**. For commenting, you can choose from the installed commenting systems. If you are using **Community Builder** or other such components, then the profiles can be used from that component.

From the **Synchronization** tab, you can set when the synchronization between local videos and that on `infinovision.com` will take place. Some hosts, such as GoDaddy, do not allow the use of the Infinovision SOAP library. In this case, a proxy can be configured from the **Proxy** tab. Similarly, from the **SEO** tab, you can set whether you want to use search engine friendly URLs or not. If yes, then what will the file extensions be. When search engine friendly URLs are enabled, video titles and other metadata are used for generating the SEF URLs.

Click on the **Categories Manager** link, and you can see the **Categories** screen, as shown in the following screenshot:

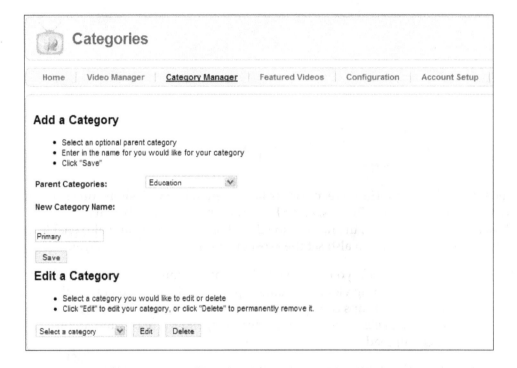

In the **Categories** screen, you can select one parent category from the predefined list, and then type the name of the new category. You can also edit an existing category name from this screen.

Click on the **Account Setup** link, which opens the **Account Setup** screen, as shown in the next screenshot, to configure your account information for `infinovision.com`. You need to create an account at `infinovision.com` to use their API and video system. If you use the professional version and pay for it, then the video player can be branded for your site. You don't need to pay for the free version, but you do need to get a free account. The account can be created for a specific domain, and a single account cannot be used for multiple domains.

Once the account information is entered and saved, click on the **Dashboard** link. That will load the dashboard from where you can brand the video player for your site.

Adding videos to your site

In JVideo! you can upload existing videos or directly record a video if you have a webcam installed. When you upload a video, the uploaded video is never stored on your web server. Instead, it is uploaded to `infinovision.com` and is converted into the streaming media format. Thus, it allows you to reduce the load on your web server, especially by saving a lot of disk space.

To upload a video to this media stream, click on the **Video Manager** link. This shows the **Video Manager** screen, as shown in the following screenshot:

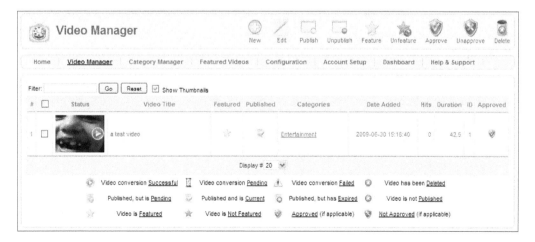

If you have already uploaded videos to this site, then the videos will be listed on this screen. You can see the status of the video and also change its status, for example, publish or unpublish, approve or disapprove. To add a new video, click on the **New** icon on the toolbar which brings up the video uploader in the **Add a Video** screen, as shown in the following screenshot:

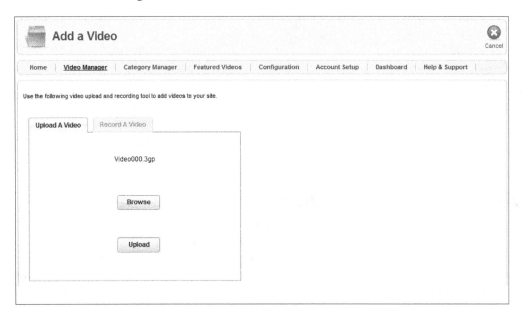

Click on the **Browse** button to select a video, and then click on the **Upload** button to start uploading the selected video. A progress bar will be displayed when the upload starts. Once the video has been uploaded, you will be redirected to the **Add a Video** form to enter information about the uploaded video, as shown in the following screenshot:

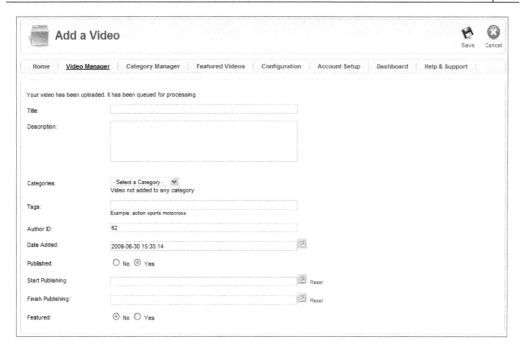

Fill in this form with the title, description, category, tags, publishing date, and so on for the uploaded video. You can choose whether the uploaded video will be featured or not. When you are done filling up this form, click on the **Save** icon on the toolbar and you will be taken to the **Video Manager** screen. This screen will show the newly added video listed. You can select the video, approve, and publish it using this screen.

Showing videos in the frontend

Once you have added the desired videos to the videos gallery, you need to display the listing of these videos in the frontend so that visitors to your site can view them. To publish a listing of the available videos, download and install the JVideo! module. Once installed, go to **Extensions | Module Manager** and click on **JVideo! Module**. This will show the **Module: [Edit]** screen for the JVideo! module, as shown in the following screenshot:

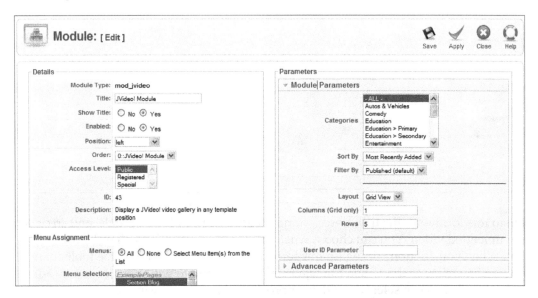

As usual, from the **Details** section, provide a title for the module, enable it, set the order of display, set an access level, and assign the menus from where it will be visible. The module-specific settings are in the **Parameters** section. From **Module Parameters**, select the categories to be displayed, the order of sorting, the filtering, the layout, the number of rows and columns, and how the User ID is configured. You can define some more settings by clicking on **Advanced Parameters,** as shown in the following screenshot:

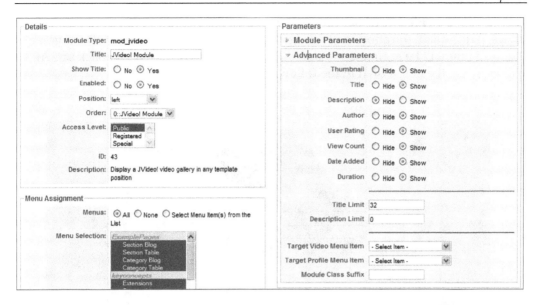

As you can see, you can configure a lot of parameters from the **Advanced Parameters** section. Once you have configured all these parameters, save the settings by clicking on the **Save** icon on the toolbar. Now, preview the site, and you will find the module populated with the videos you have added. The module will look as shown in the following screenshot:

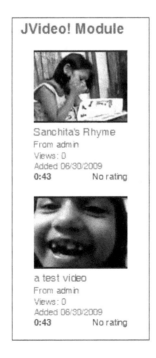

As you see, the videos are listed with thumbnails, titles, author names, number of views, date added, duration, and rating information. Click on any thumbnail you like, and you will be redirected to that video playback. The video playback screen will look like the one shown in the following screenshot:

In the playback screen, you also get a link URL to that page and a code for embedding that video. The users logged in to the site can also rate the video.

Besides using this module to display the list of videos, you can also create a menu item for the JVideo! component, through which users can access the JVideo! component. To do so, click on the menu item, and this will display the component page, as shown in this screenshot:

Video Gallery

Sanchita's Rhyme
From admin
Views: 1
Added 06/30/2009
0:43   No rating

a test video
From admin
Views: 0
Added 06/30/2009
0:43   No rating

Powered by JVideo - Joomla Video

Adding videos to content

You can also add videos to content using the JVideo Content plugin. After downloading and installing this plugin, enable it from **Extensions | Plugin Manager**. Once the plugin is enabled, you can embed a video in any Joomla! article or some other content using the following syntax:

```
{jvideo id=[int] height=[int] width=[int] autoPlay=[bool]
   allowFullScreen=[bool]}
```

You only need to know the ID of the video you want to embed. Optionally, you can specify the height and width in pixels, whether it will be autoplayed or not, and if a fullscreen view will be allowed. Now, if we want to embed a video uploaded earlier, then the following code has to be inserted in the article text:

```
{jvideo id=1 height=400 width=500 autoPlay=0}
```

This will show the video embedded, as shown in the following screenshot:

If you use `autoPlay=1`, then the playback will start after buffering the video.

As with the content plugin, you can also install and use the JVideo! Search plugin, which allows you to search for JVideo! content.

 For more information on JVideo! and to download the JVideo! component, modules, and plugins, please visit `http://jvideo.infinovision.com`.

Adding Flash MP3 players

There are several extensions for Joomla! with which you can embed Flash-based MP3 players into your Joomla! site. Embedding such MP3 players allows the visitors to play MP3 songs on your site. Some extensions allow you to upload and build MP3 collectors. Now we will be looking at some of these extensions for Joomla!.

Simple MP3 Bar

Simple MP3 Bar is a simple module that can display a Flash MP3 player on your site and can play one or more MP3 files from a specified folder on your web server. You don't need to prepare a playlist for this module. This module is licensed under **GPL (General Public License)** and is freely available for download at `http://code.google.com/p/simple-mp3-bar/downloads/list`. Once downloaded and installed, go to **Extensions | Module Manager**, and click on the **Simple MP3 Bar** module. That opens up the **Module: [Edit]** screen for the **Simple MP3 Bar** module, as shown in the following screenshot:

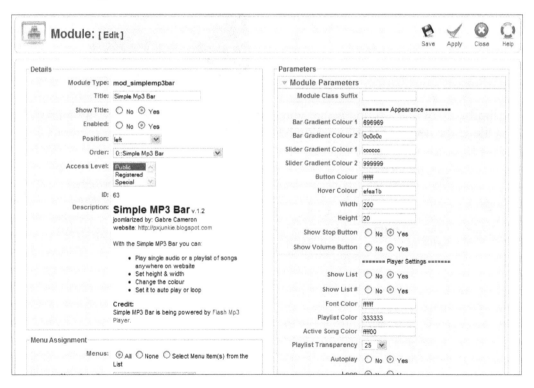

In the **Details** section, provide a title for the module, enable the module, select a position, and the order of display for the module. The module-specific settings are in the **Parameters** section. Among other settings, you can specify the gradient colors, the button color, the width, and the height of the Flash MP3 player. You can also specify whether the stop and the volume buttons will be shown or not, whether autoplay will be enabled or not, whether looping will be enabled or not, and so on. An important setting in this section is whether it will play a single file or play from a playlist. Specify the path for the folder from which the MP3 files will be played. You need to upload your MP3 files in this folder. For example, if you keep the MP3 files in the /images/songs folder, then type this path into the **Folder** field. In the **File(s)** field, type the names of the MP3 files you want to play. This list may contain multiple names separated by commas (,). If you want to display the titles of the songs, then you can type a comma separated list in the **Song Titles** field. When published, the module will look as shown in the following screenshot:

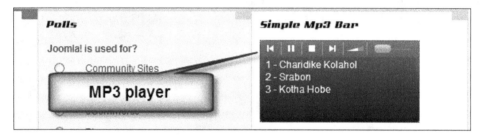

The limitation of this module is that you don't get an interface for uploading an MP3 file to the designated folder. You have to upload files using other methods such as FTP.

You can use the Joomla! Media Manager for uploading MP3 files to the images/songs folder. However, you need to add the .mp3 extension in the **Legal Extensions (File Types)** field in the **Site | Global Configuration | System** screen. Moreover, you may need to set a suitable value in the php.ini file for the maximum file upload size to allowthe uploading of MP3 files.

UnMP3 for Joomla! 1.5

The unMP3 extension allows you to upload MP3 files to your web server and to edit a playlist and publish it through the unMP3 module. This freely available extension is available for download at `http://www.unmp3.com/unmp3_download.html`. Download both the component and the module, and install these from the **Extensions | Install/Uninstall** screen. Once installed, you can configure this component by selecting **Components | unMP3**. This shows the **unMP3** screen, as shown in the following screenshot:

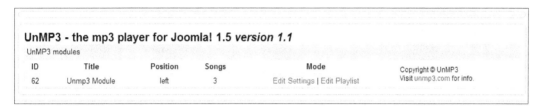

The **UnMP3** screen lists the available configured modules. You can edit the settings for this component by clicking on the **Edit Settings** link, which displays the screen, as shown in the next screenshot:

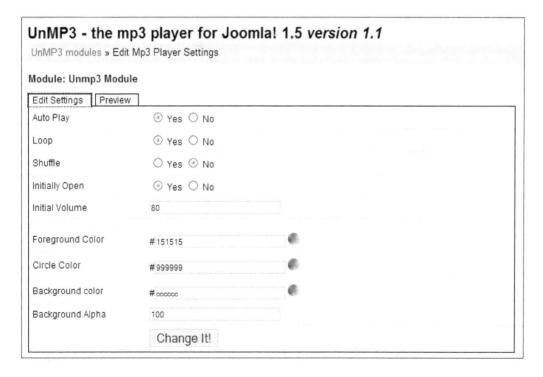

You can specify whether autoplay, looping, shuffling, and initial opening will be on or off. You can also specify values for the initial volume, foreground color, circle color, background color, and background alpha from this screen. After changing this, click on the **Preview** tab to see how the player looks. It should appear like the one shown in the following screenshot:

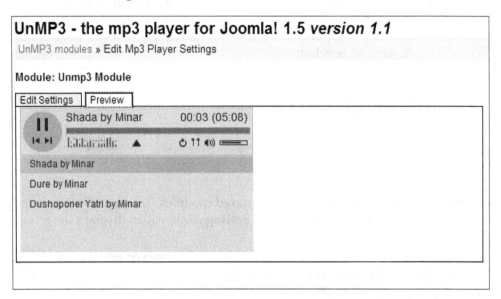

To upload MP3 songs and to edit the playlist, click on the **Edit Playlist** link in the **UnMp3** screen. This shows the file upload dialog box, as shown in the following screenshot:

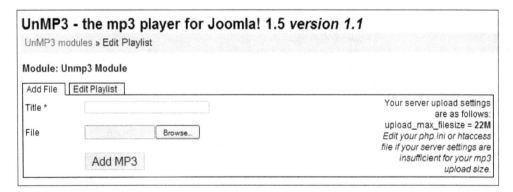

Type a title for the song in the **Title** field, and click on the **Browse** button to select the song you want to upload. Once you have selected the song to be uploaded, click on the **Add MP3** button to upload the MP3 file. Once the song has been uploaded, you can edit the playlist by clicking on the **Edit Playlist** tab, as shown in the following screenshot:

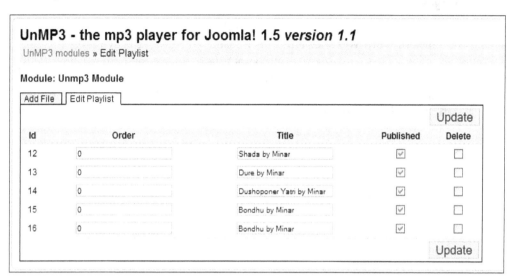

In this playlist editor screen, you can set the order in which the songs will play, edit the titles, publish or unpublish the songs, and delete selected songs. Once this is done, click on **Update** to save the changes.

To display the Flash MP3 player, you need to install and publish the UnMP3 module using **Extensions | Module Manager**. When you preview the frontend now, the player will appear as shown in the following screenshot:

As you can see, the titles specified are displayed below the player controls. You can select any of the titles listed, and the selected title starts playing in the MP3 player. You can use multiple modules to show several playlists in different positions as well.

Flash MP3 Player

Flash MP3 Player is a simple but powerful module for Joomla! that can be used for playing MP3 files on your website. This Flash-based MP3 player is available for download at `http://www.gutierrez.nu/downloads/files/mod_mp3playerJ15v-1-3-2en.zip`. After downloading the file and installing it, go to **Extensions | Module Manager**. Then click on the **Flash MP3 Player** module, which opens up the **Module: [Edit]** screen for the **Flash Mp3 Player** module, as shown in the following screenshot:

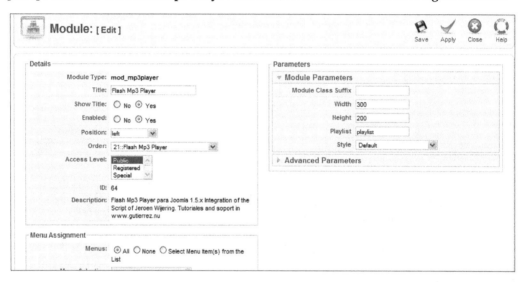

From the **Details** section, provide a title for the module, select **Yes** or **No** in the **Show Title** field, enable the module by selecting **Yes** in the **Enabled** field, select a position for the module, and set an access level for the module.

The module-specific settings are in the **Parameters** section. Click on **Module Parameters** and specify the **Height, Width, Playlist**, and **Style** parameters for the player. The playlist is an XML file. You should type the filename of the playlist excluding the `.xml` extension. For example, if you want to use the playlist named `modern.xml`, then type modern in the **Playlist** field. The playlist remains in the `/modules/mod_mp3player/files/` folder. The structure of the playlist file is as follows:

```
<?xml version="1.0" encoding="UTF-8" ?>
<playlist version="1" xmlns="http://xspf.org/ns/0/">
    <title>Sample XSPF Playlist</title>
```

```
<info>http://www.suhreedsarkar.com/jflash</info>
<trackList>

  <track>
     <location>http://www.suhreedsarkar.com/jflash/modules/mod_
                       mp3player/files/mp3/jazzalude.mp3</location>
     <info>http://www.suhreedsarkar.com/</info>
     <image>http://www.suhreedsarkar.com/jflash/modules/mod_
                       mp3player/files/mp3/cover.jpg</image>
  </track>

  <track>
     <annotation>Postmen - Homeland</annotation>
     <location>http://www.suhreedsarkar.com/jflash/modules/mod_
                       mp3player/files/mp3/homeland.mp3</location>
     <info>http://geek-team.net</info>
  </track>

  <track>
     <annotation>Basement Jaxx - Jazzalude</annotation>
     <location>http://www.suhreedsarkar.com/jflash/modules/mod_
                       mp3player/files/mp3/jazzalude.mp3</location>
  </track>
</trackList>
</playlist>
```

Using the XML playlist file, you can specify the title of the song, its location URL, its information URL, the URL of the cover image, and so on. You can create multiple playlist files and attach each playlist file to one instance of the Flash MP3 Player module.

In the **Style** drop-down list, you can choose from five options: **Default, Autostart – Random, Autostart – No Random, No Autostart – Random,** and **No Autostart – No Random**.

In the **Advanced Parameters** section, you can specify whether to show **MP3 Player, Image Popup**, or **Both**. Then specify a background color for the popup and the popup image.

When configured and published, the module will look as shown in the following screenshot:

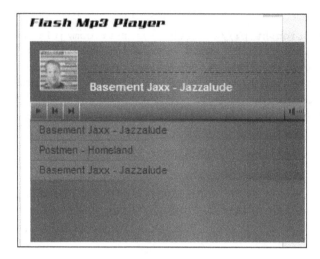

If you have selected **Autostart – Random** or **Autostart – No Random** in the **Style** drop-down list, then the player will start playing a song upon loading of the player.

Visual mind mapping with Joom!FreeMind

Mind mapping is a technique for expressing your concept in a visually pleasing way, showing the interrelation of thoughts. If you have ever seen a mind map, then you may be tempted to use it for showing your site's structure. In Joomla! 1.5, you can visually show your site's structure through a mind map. For drawing and displaying such mind maps, an extension called Joom!FreeMind is made available under the GPL license. You can download the latest version of Joom!FreeMind from `http://www.dcos.ro/en/joomfreemind.html`.

Once downloaded and installed, you can configure this extension from
Components | Joom!FreeMind. Selecting this menu shows the screen as shown
in the following screenshot:

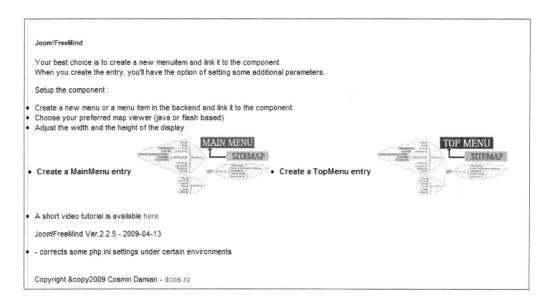

As you can see, there are two options. You can create a main menu entry or create
a top menu entry. The idea of creating a menu item is that you either create a menu
item in the main menu or in the top menu so that you can access Joom!FreeMind
and view the mind map created based on your site's structure.

To create a main menu entry, click on the **Main Menu** image. It displays a form, as shown in the following screenshot:

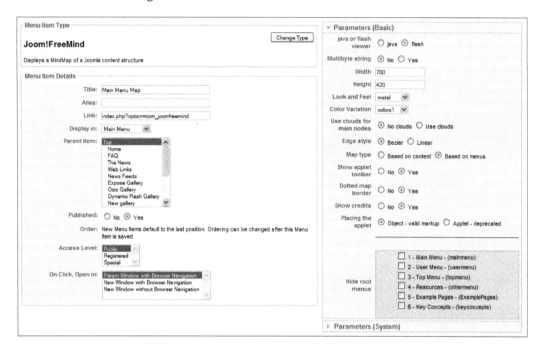

From the **Menu Item Details** section, you can provide a title for the menu, select the menu in which it will be displayed, select its parent menu, set access level, and set how it opens. The actual configuration for Joom!FreeMind is in the **Parameters (Basic)** section.

In the **Parameters (Basic)** section, you first select the kind of viewer that you want to use—**java** or **flash**. Select **flash** in the **java or flash viewer** field. To convert characters using mbstring, you have to select **Yes** in the **Multibyte String** field. In this case, your PHP should be enabled with mbstring. Do not enable **Multibyte String** unless you understand what it means and how to use mbstring.

Here you can set the width, the height, the look and feel, and the color variation of the Flash viewer. You can also set the edge style and map type. Maps can be based on the content in your site or based on menus. Finally, you can exclude any root menu from the analysis and mind map.

When the configurations and the menu item are saved, preview the site. You see the menu item on the main menu. Click on the menu item, and you see the mind map of your site, as shown in the following screenshot:

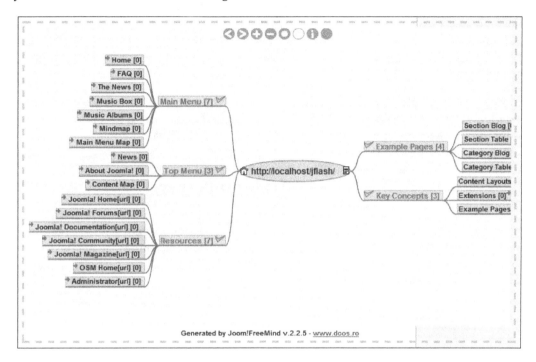

As you can see, the menus are displayed on this map. You also see the menu items inside the menus. Clicking on a menu icon in this map hides or unhides the items. On the top of the map, you see the mind map controls. You can zoom in or zoom out, scroll left or right, and resize the map from these controls. This kind of mind map can be useful in displaying the site structure to the visitors.

Summary

In this chapter, we have explored many Joomla! extensions which add different functionalities to our website. We have seen how to use YOS amMap and YOS amChart to create and display interactive Flash-based maps and charts. We have learned about using sIFR with Joomla! to display Joomla! content in fonts that are not installed on users' computers. We have also seen how to use the Flash uploader on a Joomla! site.

There are several good Flash-based video and MP3 players that can be used with a Joomla! website. We have seen how to use the JVideo! extension to embed videos in Joomla! content and transform your Joomla! site into a streaming media site. You have also learned about using some MP3 players, which allows you to play MP3 files on your site using Flash-based MP3 players. At the end, we have seen how to use the Joom!FreeMind component for creating a mind map based on the structure of a Joomla! site.

With these skills of selecting and using different extensions for Joomla! to serve your purpose, we will move on to more complex uses of Flash in Joomla!. In the next chapter, we will look at changing the look and feel of a Joomla! site by using Flash with Joomla! templates, headers, and banners.

6
Flash Decorations: Flashy Templates, Headers, Banners, and Tickers

So far we have seen how to use Flash for enhancing our content by adding Flash animations, charts, maps, movies, videos, and sound clips. We have not yet used it to change the decoration of our site though. In this chapter, we are going to use Flash for decorating our site. On completion of this chapter you will be able to use:

- Flash-based templates for your Joomla! website
- Flash logos
- Flash headers
- Flash banners

In this chapter, we will mainly focus on the visual design of our site. To acquire the information presented here, it is assumed that you have some basic understanding of Joomla!'s visual design including templates, components, module position, and so on.

Adding Flash in templates

If you are familiar with Joomla! templates, then you will understand that there are two ways to display Flash in a template:

- By hardcoded embedding of Flash items
- By dynamically loading Flash objects at module positions

We have seen many modules that can display Flash objects. Therefore, in this section, we will be looking into the embedding of Flash objects within templates. It will also be helpful if we understand the structure of Joomla! templates.

Generally templates for Joomla! include headers in Flash. Flash animations are included in the header area of a Joomla! template. Some templates include the mechanism to show images from a specific directory. For example, the template shown in the following screenshot, available for download at `http://joomlatp.com/joomla-1.5-templates/Templates-has-flash-header.html`, is designed to show a Flash header comprised of the images kept in a directory:

The following sections briefly describe the structure of a Joomla! template and the ways to embed a Flash object in this template.

Structure of a Joomla! template

The look and feel of Joomla! is determined by templates. You can apply a template to the frontend as well as to the backend. Templates for the Joomla! frontend reside in the `/templates` directory of the Joomla! webroot, while those for the administration panel are found in the `/administrator/templates` directory. You can install multiple templates and apply one or more templates to the different sections. However, you must designate one default template for the site.

To designate a default template, go to **Extensions | Template Manager**. Select the desired template and click on the **Default** button on the toolbar. For assigning a template to a specific section of the site, click on a template, except the default template, and then select the section or the menu item for which you want to assign the template from the **Menu Assignment** section.

If you examine the directory structure of a Joomla! template, you will find at least the following subdirectories in the templates directory:

Directory	Description
mx_joofree2	This is the main template directory. It contains some subdirectories and at least the following files under its root: <ul><li>index.php: This is the main file for a template. The basic structure of a Joomla! template is defined in this file. We will examine this file later.</li><li>templateDetails.xml: This XML file defines the template by mentioning its designer, the different files bundled with it, the positions and parameters available, and so on.</li><li>params.ini: This file contains the parameters and their default values. For example, a template may use several colors for theming, but users can select a preferred color as a parameter for this template, and that information is stored in this file.</li></ul>
mx_joofree2/css	This directory contains all the cascading stylesheets to be used for a Joomla! site. This directory will contain at least one stylesheet named template_css.css. It may also contain a stylesheet named template_ie6.css and other stylesheets.
mx_joofree2/html	This folder may contain some definitions for the custom rendering of certain parts of the site. For example, the mx_joofree2 template contains two files—module.php and pagination.php. These two files define custom module rendering and pagination for Joomla!. For more information on using HTML overrides, refer to http://docs.joomla.org/How_to_override_the_content_from_the_Joomla!_core.
mx_joofree2/images	This folder contains the images for the template. It may contain a logo image, a background image, and so on. It may also contain some subdirectories, for example, the mx_joofree2 template contains a subdirectory images/headers, where the header images for the template are stored.

As you know, the main structure of a Joomla! template is defined in the `index.php` file. The file looks as follows:

```
<?php
// no direct access
defined( '_JEXEC' ) or die( 'Restricted index access' );
```

This line of code is to prevent direct access to the file. This is a convention to prevent direct access to any file in Joomla!. After this, the following lines define some variables for the template that will be used later on in the template:

```
define( 'YOURBASEPATH', dirname(__FILE__) );
$live_site               = $mainframe->getCfg('live_site');
$template_path           = $this->baseurl . '/templates/' .
                                             $this->template;
$show_flashheader        = ($this->params->get("showFlashheader",
                                    1) == 0)?"false":"true";
$show_logo               = ($this->params->get("showLogo", 1) ==
                                    0)?"false":"true";
$show_date               = ($this->params->get("showDate", 1) ==
                                    0)?"false":"true";
$show_breadcrumbs        = ($this->params->get("showBreadcrumbs",
                                    1) == 0)?"false":"true";
?>
```

Having defined the template variables, the template's structure starts with some common HTML declarations as follows:

```
<!DOCTYPE html PUBLIC "-//W3C//DTD XHTML 1.0 Transitional//EN"
  "http://www.w3.org/TR/xhtml1/DTD/xhtml1-transitional.dtd">
<html xmlns="http://www.w3.org/1999/xhtml" xml:lang="<?php echo
  $this->language; ?>" lang="<?php echo $this->language; ?>" >
<head>
```

Whatever is included after the following lines will be considered as included in the `<head>` section. Generally, stylesheets, JavaScript, and site-wide files are included in a template's `<head>` section with the following lines:

```
<jdoc:include type="head" />

<link rel="shortcut icon" href="<?php echo $this->baseurl; ?>/images/
favicon.ico" />
<link href="<?php echo $this->baseurl ?>/templates/system/
      css/system.css" rel="stylesheet" type="text/css" />
<link href="<?php echo $this->baseurl ?>/templates/system/css/general.
      css" rel="stylesheet" type="text/css" />
<link href="<?php echo $this->baseurl; ?>/templates/<?php echo
      $this->template?>/css/template_css.css" rel="stylesheet"
      type="text/css" />
```

```
<!--[if lte IE 6]>
<link rel="stylesheet" href="templates/<?php echo $this->template ?>
    /css/ie6.css" type="text/css" />
<![endif]-->

</head>
```

Next, the body section of the template starts:

```
<body class="body_bg">
<div id="bgr">

<div id="wrapper">
<div id="tophead">
```

The following block checks whether any module for position user4 is enabled. If the count of enabled modules is greater than zero, then a <div> element with an ID search is displayed, and modules specified for position user4 are displayed as children of this <div> element:

```
<?php if($this->countModules('user4')) : ?>
<div id="search">
<jdoc:include type="modules" name="user4" style="xhtml" />
</div>
<?php endif; ?>
```

Having placed the modules for the position user4, the following block now defines where to show the site's logo. This block of code dynamically selects the site's logo and links that to the site's home page:

```
<!-- BEGIN: LOGO -->
<?php if($show_logo == "true") : ?>
<div id="logo">
<a href="<?php echo $mosConfig_live_site;?>">
<img src="<?php echo $this->baseurl; ?>/templates/<?php echo
    $this->template?>/images/logo.png" alt="" />
</a>
</div>
<?php endif; ?>
<!-- END: LOGO -->
```

If we want to show a Flash header beside the logo, then we can add the following block to include a Flash object:

```
<!-- BEGIN: flashheader -->
<?php if($show_flashheader == "true") : ?>
<div id="ol-flashheader">
```

```
<object type="application/x-shockwave-flash" data="<?php echo
        $this->baseurl; ?>/templates/<?php echo $this->template?>/
        images/header.swf " width="700" height="240">
<param name="wmode" value="transparent" />
<param name="movie" value="<?php echo $this->baseurl; ?>/templates/
   <?php echo $this->template?>/images/header.swf" />
</object>

</div>
<?php endif; ?>
<!-- END: flashheader -->
```

This code block first checks whether the variable for showing a Flash header is checked or not. If it is checked, then a `<div>` element will be created, under which the Flash object is embedded using the `<object>` `</object>` tags.

The following code block is used to display the current date on the site:

```
<!-- BEGIN: Date -->
<?php if($show_date == "true") : ?>
<div id="date-format">
<?php $now = &JFactory::getDate(); echo $now->toFormat("%A, %d %b
                                                        %Y"); ?>
</div>
<?php endif; ?>
<!-- END: Date -->
</div>
```

The following block defines another module position. Modules designated for the user3 position will be displayed here. Note that modules are included with the `<jdoc:include type="modules" name="position-name" />` markup:

```
<?php if( $this->countModules('user3') ) {?>
<div id="topcol">
<div id="topmenu">
<table cellspacing="0" cellpadding="0" style="float: left;">
<tr>
<td>
<jdoc:include type="modules" name="user3" />
</td>
</tr>
</table>
</div>
</div>
<?php } ?>
<div id="wrapper_2">
<div id="holder">
```

The following code block displays another module called breadcrumbs. First, it checks whether the parameter is set to show breadcrumbs or not. If it is, then the breadcrumbs module will be displayed in the block:

```
<!--pathway start-->
  <?php if ($show_breadcrumbs == "true") : ?>
<div class="path">
  You are here: <jdoc:include type="module" name="breadcrumbs"/>
</div>
<?php endif; ?>
<!--pathway end-->
```

Next comes the module for the left position:

```
<div id="content">
  <?php if($this->countModules('left') and
JRequest::getCmd('layout') != 'form') : ?>
<div id="left">
  <jdoc:include type="modules" name="left" style="rounded" />
</div>
<?php endif; ?>
```

The following block includes the modules designated for the right position:

```
<?php if($this->countModules('right') and JRequest::getCmd('layout')
                                         != 'form') : ?>
<div id="main">
<?php else: ?>
<div id="main_full">
<?php endif; ?>
<div class="nopad">
<jdoc:include type="message" />
```

The next code block counts the number of modules available for the user1 and user2 positions and then includes the modules designated for these two positions. Note the highlighted line of code in this code block. It shows the component currently selected:

```
<!-- BEGIN: USERS TEMPSPLASH -->
<div id="lr-padd">
<table class="lr-padd" cellspacing="2">
<tr valign="top">
  <?php if ( $this->countModules('user1') ) {?>
<td class="lr-padd">
  <jdoc:include type="modules" name="user2" style="xhtml" />
</td>
```

```php
<?php } ?>
<?php if( $this->countModules('user1') ) {?>
<td class="lr-padd">
<jdoc:include type="modules" name="user2" style="xhtml" />
</td>
<?php } ?>
</tr>
</table>

</div>
<!-- END: USERS TEMPSPLASH -->
<jdoc:include type="component" />
</div>
</div>

<?php if($this->countModules('right') and JRequest::getCmd('layout')
!= 'form') : ?>
<div id="right">
<jdoc:include type="modules" name="right" style="rounded" />
</div>
<?php endif; ?>
<div class="clr"></div>
</div>
</div>
```

Finally, here comes the footer section. The highlighted line in the following code block includes a footer file to show the footer text:

```php
<!--footer start-->
<div id="footer">
<div id="footer_in">
<div>
<div style="text-align: center; padding: 18px 0 0;">
<?php include (dirname(__FILE__).DS.'/footer.php');?>
</div>
</div>
</div>
</div>
<!--footer end-->
</div>
</div>
</div>
</div>
<jdoc:include type="modules" name="debug" />
</body>
</html>
```

All this code in the `index.php` file when rendered with `template_css.css` and other stylesheets will display a layout like the one shown in the following screenshot:

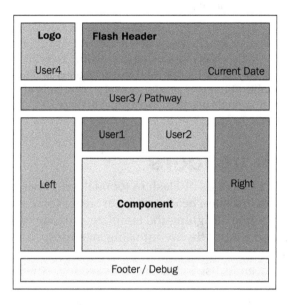

In a Joomla! template, the site's data comes from the database and fits in different positions. When you are planning for Flash-based Joomla! templates, you should first identify where to put the Flash objects and where to display the dynamic data for the site. In the template layout, we have seen that a suitable place for adding a Flash object are the logo and the header positions. We can also use some extensions to display Flash headers. The following sections explain how to use extensions for showing Flash logos and headers.

Using Flash logos

A logo is a special graphic displayed at a specific position on the Joomla! template. You can replace the ordinary image with Flash-animated logos by embedding it in that position. As we have seen earlier, Flash objects are embedded in Joomla! templates using the `<object> </object>` XHTML element. For styling purposes, you may put this element under a `<div>` element, as shown in the following code:

```
<div id="logo">
  <object type="application/x-shockwave-flash"
          data="/templates/mx_joofree2/images/logo.swf"
          width="200" height="200">
<param name="movie" value="/templates/mx_joofree2/images/logo.swf">
  </object>
</div>
```

As you can see, the `<object>` `</object>` tag can contain child elements. We pass parameters to the Flash objects using the `<param>` element. For example, we have passed the name of a movie file using the highlighted tag in the previous code.

 Some of you may already know about the SWFObject JavaScript library. It is used to embed Flash files using JavaScript. You can also use it to embed Flash objects in Joomla! and can also generate Flash objects. It is freely available at `http://code.google.com/p/swfobject/`. Brief documentation on its usage is also available there.

Using Flash headers

We have seen that one of the uses of Flash in Joomla! templates is as a header. By using a Flash animation in a site's header you can create some stunning effects. As we have already seen, while designing the template, we may embed Flash animation in the header region and control the layout using an appropriate CSS stylesheet. To embed such Flash animations like these, you can use the `<object>` `</object>` XHTML tag. We have seen its use in the previous section. An alternative to this is showing the Flash header at some module position. There are several extensions that can be used for showing Flash objects at a module position. We will be looking at some of them next.

Using Flexheader3

Flexheader3 is a Joomla! 1.5-compatible extension for using Flash as headers in Joomla! sites. This is available for download for free at `http://flexheader2.andrehotzler.de/en/download/folder/208-flexheader3.html`. After downloading the package, install it from the **Extensions | Install/Uninstall** screen in Joomla! administration. Then click on **Extensions | Module Manager**. In the **Module Manager** screen, you will find the module named **Flexheader3**. Click on it and that shows the **Module: [Edit]** screen for the Flexheader3 module, as shown in the following screenshot:

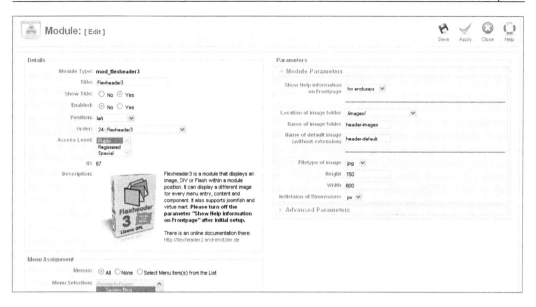

The **Details** section is similar to other modules from where you enable the module, select the module position to display this, select the order of display, and assign menus for which this module will be displayed. The module-specific settings are in the **Parameters** section. As you see, selecting the module position is crucial for this module. Most of the templates don't have a position to display the header using a module. Therefore, you may need to create a module position for displaying a Flash header. The following section shows you how to create a module position displaying a header.

Creating a module position

To create a module position in your template you need to edit at least two files. Browse to the /templates directory, and click on the name of the template that you want to modify. You need to edit two files in the template folder: index.php and templateDetails.xml. First, open the templateDetails.xml file in your text editor and find the <positions> tag. Under this, type the line highlighted in the following code so that the file looks like the following:

```
<positions>
    <position>flexheader</position>
    <position>left</position>
    <position>user1</position>
    . . .
    <position>right</position>
    <position>debug</position>
</positions>
```

Remember to type `<position>flexheader</position>` before ending `</positions>` tag. Placing it outside the `<positions> </positions>` block will make the template unusable.

After modifying the `templateDetails.xml` file, open the `index.php` file in your text editor. Find out the code for including a header image in that template. Generally, this is done by inserting an image using the `<img src=... />` tag. If you don't find such a tag, then look for `<div id="header" ...>` or something like that. In such cases, CSS is used to display the background image to the `div` element.

Once you have found the code for showing the header image, replace it with the following code:

```
<jdoc:include type="modules" name="flexheader" style="RAW" />
```

This line of code means that you are instructing to include modules designated for the `flexheader` position. When we assign the Flexheader3 module to this position, the contents of that module will be displayed in this position. Generally, this module will produce a code like the following in this position:

```
<img src="/images/header.png"
    title="My header image"
    alt="Header image"
    style="width: 528px; height: 70px;"
/>
```

When changes to `index.php` are made, save those changes. We will be configuring the module to display a Flash header in this module position.

Configuring the module

After creating a module position for Flexheader by modifying the `index.php` and `templateDetails.xml` files, you can configure the Flexheader3 module to show the Flash header. To configure the Flexheader3 module, go to the **Parameters** section in the **Module: [Edit]** screen for the Flexheader3 module. Now we will look into the **Module Parameters** section shown in the following screenshot:

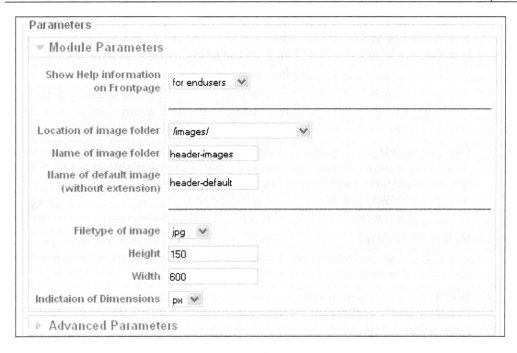

In the **Module Parameters** section you need to configure the following:

- **Show Help information on Frontpage**: When showing Flash headers you may display some help tips for the frontend users. You can choose:
    - **none** — to prevent showing such help
    - **for endusers** — if you want to show help to site visitors
    - **for developers** — if you want to show help messages to developers only.

    Selecting **for developers** is logical as that enables the messages and fixing if needed.

- **Location of image folder**: Select the path of the folder where you have stored the images to be displayed in the header. You can select /images or /templates/current template. Selecting /images stores the header images in the global /images directory, which can then be accessed through the media manager. On the other hand, you can store the images into the template's images folder. In such a case, select the /templates/current template/ option from the drop-down list.

- **Name of image folder**: Specify the name of the folder where the header images will be stored. If you have selected /images in the previous field and type **header-images** in this field, then the images will be stored in the /images/header_images folder.

- **Name of default image (without extension)**: Type the name of the default image to be displayed if there is no image. Specify the name without the file extension; extensions for the images will be defined later.

- **Filetype of image**: Specify the type of images used for the header. You need to select an extension from the drop-down list. The available extensions are: **jpg, jpeg, gif**, and **png**. Remember that when you select an extension the images to be used for the header have to be of that type. If you select **png**, for example, the header images need to be in the PNG format.

- **Height**: Specify the height of the header images in pixels or percentage, as indicated in the **Indication of Dimensions** field. All images need to be resized to this height.

- **Width**: Specify the width of the header images in pixels or percentage, as indicated in the **Indication of Dimensions** field. All images need to be the same width as this.

- **Indication of Dimensions**: Select either **px** or **%** to indicate the unit of dimension. For example, if you select **px** in this drop-down list, the values in the **Height** and **Width** fields will be in pixels. For a fluid layout you may specify the image height and width in percentage. In this case, you have to select % from the drop-down list.

You can display images, XHTML <div>, or Flash objects using the Flexheader3 module. The **Advanced Parameters** section for the module, shown in the next screenshot, allows you to configure what will be displayed in this module and how:

▷ Module Parameters

▽ Advanced Parameters

Display mode   [Image ▼]

DIV Content (for Display mode=DIV Area with background image)   [   ]

IMG Alternative Text (XHTML ALT)   [   ]

Hyperlinked header   ⦿ No   ○ Yes

Hyperlink Target   [/]

JoomFish Support   ⦿ No   ○ Yes

VirtueMart Support   ⦿ No   ○ Yes

Load a css file   ⦿ No   ○ Yes

Position of Debug information   [On bottom of frontpage ▼]

Debug Background Color   [Red ▼]

Debug Opacity   [80 ▼]

Debug Height   [auto ▼]

Module Class Suffix   [   ]

Flexheader3 CSS Class   [   ]

Caching   [Use Global ▼]

Cache Time   [900]

From the **Advanced Parameters** section you need to configure the following:

- **Display Mode**: Select a display mode from this drop-down list. You can either display an image, a `<div>` object, or a Flash object with this module. Select any one from the drop-down list: **Image**, **DIV area with image as background**, or **Flash Object**. One of the reasons you may want to use `<div>` is that you want to show some text in the header. When you use a `<div>`, images are used as background to the `<div>` tag and the text inside the `<div>` tag is visible. Based on the selection of this field, you need to configure the other fields.

- **DIV Content (for Display mode=DIV Area with background image)**: When you have selected **DIV Area with background image** in the **Display Mode** field, you need to specify the DIV content in this textbox. For example, if you want to display the logo in the header, then simply type `<img src="/templates/mx_joofree2/images/logo.png" />` and the logo will be displayed as an overlay to the header images. However, for formatting the DIV content, you also need to specify the relevant styles in the CSS file.

- **IMG Alternative Text (XHTML ALT)**: When you select **Image** in the **Display Mode** field to display images in the Flexheader3 module, you can specify alternative text for images, which is equivalent to the `alt` attribute in the `<img>` tag.

- **Hyperlinked header**: You can make the header hyperlinked. If you want to make it hyperlinked, then select **Yes** for this field.

- **Hyperlink Target**: If you have selected **Yes** for the **Hyperlinked header** field, then specify the URL for the hyperlink in this field. This URL may be relative or absolute.

- **JoomFish Support**: Flexheader3 can display language-specific images. For example, your site has two languages—English (en), and French (fr). You create the language-specific header images, such as `1-en.png`, `2-en.png`, `3-en.png`, `4-en.png`, and so on for English, and `1-fr.png`, `2-fr.png`, `3-fr.png`, `4-fr.png`, and so on for French. Then, to enable the multilingual feature, select **Yes** in the **JoomFish Support** field.

- **VirtueMart Support**: Prefixing the image names with the VirtueMart category and product IDs, such as `category1_product1_01.png`, may link that image to that category and product. To enable this support for linking with VirtueMart products and categories, select **Yes** in this field.

- **Load a css file**: Select **Yes** to use a CSS file for formatting different pages.

- **Position of Debug Information**: Specify the position where you want the debug information for this Flexheader3 module to be displayed. You can show this on top or at the bottom of the front page. This will be very useful for adjusting the module's output.

- **Debug Background Color**: Specify a background color for the debug information shown on the front page. You can select Red, Blue, Yellow, Green, or Cyan as the background color for the debug information.

- **Debug Opacity**: Specify the opacity for the debug information by selecting a number from 5 to 100 from the drop-down list.

- **Debug Height**: Specify the height of the debug window as a percentage of the size of the main window. Select a percentage from the drop-down list or select **auto** to let the height be adjusted automatically.

- **Module Class Suffix**: For individual module styling, you can specify a suffix to the module class so that you can apply appropriate CSS styles to this class suffix. For example, you can specify the module suffix `myclass`, and add a CSS declaration `module-heading-myclass` to define your own style for this module's heading.

- **Flexheader3 CSS Class**: You can specify a CSS class for the Flexheader3 module. You should use such a class if you have included the Flexheader3 module as *raw*, without any styling.

- **Caching**: You can select **Use Global** from the drop-down list to enable caching for this module. Select **No caching** to disable caching.

- **Cache Time**: If you have chosen to use caching, then specify the time in minutes, after which the module will be re-cached.

If we configure these settings for the Flexheader3 module and save them, you will find the header—either images from the specified directories or SWF animations—displayed in the newly created Flexheader module position. The module will look similar to the following screenshot:

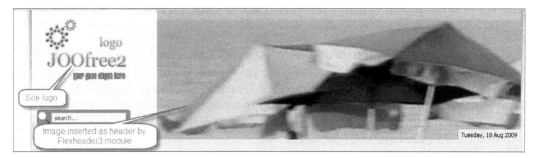

Using Web Flash Module to show headers

We have seen the use of `mod_web_flash` in Chapter 3, *Creating Attractive Menus with Flash*. There we learned how to use this module for creating menus. In fact, we can use the same thing as a site's header. The only difference will be in configuring the module differently with appropriate images, texts, and link URLs. Then we have to publish that module in a position like the Flexheader3 module position. For example, placing the same module that we had configured in Chapter 3 would display the header, as shown in the following screenshot:

When using the Web Flash Joomla 1.5 module (`mod_web_flash`), you can also add menu links to the rotating header images. It will be nice to add different background images, some text (a slogan for your site), and then linking them to the different parts of your website.

Using Flash banners

Joomla! has a banner management system from where you can add banner clients, categorize the banners, define the banners, and publish the banners through the module. Usually you can display banner images using this component and also manage the banners very effectively. You can specify the banner images and links for the same. The banners can be displayed for a specified duration or for a certain number of impressions. Unfortunately, we cannot display a Flash banner using this banner component.

For adding animated Flash banners, we need to use third-party extensions. Any module that can show a Flash object at a module location can be used to display Flash banners. For example, we have already learned how to use the Web Flash Joomla! 1.5 module. We can use this module as a banner. To do this, first create a Flash animated banner and configure the module to display this Flash object at a position called **banner** in your template.

You can always hardcode your Flash objects to a Joomla! template. In this case, Flash banners can also be displayed in a Joomla! site using the `<object> </object>` tags. However, you will have to edit the template file each time you change the banner.

Flash tickers

Tickers are used for displaying small amounts of information on your site. You can either use text-based tickers or animated Flash tickers. The same principle applies when displaying animated Flash tickers. If you want to display an animated Flash ticker, design the ticker with appropriate text, images, sounds, and so on, and publish it on your site. Like others, you can display this either by embedding the ticker Flash object in the template, or by publishing it through a module. If you want to use a module for publishing tickers, use the Web Flash Joomla! 1.5 module or any other module that can display one or more animated Flash objects from a directory on your web server.

Summary

Although Flash can be used for designing the layout of a Joomla! site, it is often used as a header or a logo for the site's template. You can use Flash objects in different parts of the Joomla! template to display the Flash objects. In this chapter, we have learned two ways of showing Flash objects in a Joomla! site: by embedding the Flash object in a Joomla! template and showing it permanently on a Joomla! website; and by using a suitable module. First, we have seen how to embed Flash objects in Joomla! templates using the `<object> </object>` tag. Later, we have explored options for displaying Flash objects using the Joomla! modules such as FlexHeader3 and Web Flash Joomla!.

In the following chapter, we are going to learn about using web services with Flash and the accessibility issues with it.

7
Playing with Code

Up until now, we have seen how to use Flash objects in Joomla! content. However, someone might want to do the reverse—inserting Joomla! content into a Flash site. Often, you may think about putting some content from your Joomla! site into a Flash object. In this chapter, we will focus on this issue. Besides that, we will be also looking into the accessibility issues with Flash.

On the completion of this chapter, you will be able to:

- Use Joomla! content in Flash objects by the use of the J-AMFPHP extension for Joomla!
- Identify and address the accessibility issues related to Flash

It is assumed that you are familiar with Flash development, especially in ActionScript and Flash Remoting.

Using Joomla! content in Flash

By now we know that the content of Joomla! is stored in databases. Whenever a user sends a request for an article to Joomla!, it retrieves the content of that article from the database. So far, we have seen how to use Flash objects in Joomla! contents, but we have yet not seen how to use the contents from Joomla! in a Flash object. Suppose, you have an existing site based on Flash, and now, you want to display Joomla! articles in that Flash site. In such a case, using dynamic contents in Flash is needed.

Using content from a database in Flash objects

Flash can read data from XML files. Therefore, the easiest way would be to extract the data from the database, convert it into an XML file, and iterate the XML file using a PHP script and feed it into Flash. Although it seems easy, another feature called **Flash Remoting** has been added to Flash, by which Flash objects can consume data from servers through a gateway service.

To consume the data from any web service, the Flash Player sends requests to a Flash Remoting Gateway. The Flash Remoting Gateway then reads the data from the server (or from any other web service on the internet) and sends back the data in the **Action Message Format** (**AMF**), a proprietary binary data format. The Flash Player then decodes the data and presents it to the users.

AMFPHP is an open source implementation of Flash Remoting that can be used with PHP for consuming web services in Flex/AIR/Flash applications. AMFPHP is available for free download at `http://amfphp.sourceforge.net`. You can get the basic documentation about AMFPHP on its website at `http://www.amfphp.org`.

Developing Flash content using J-AMFPHP

The AMFPHP libraries used for Flash Remoting in PHP are now made available for use with Joomla! 1.5 by *Anthony McLin* with the name **J-AMFPHP**. The package comes as a component and is freely available for download at `http://joomlacode.org/gf/project/jamfphp/frs`. From this location, you can download three files: `J-AMFPHPCoreComponentv0.3.2.zip`, `J-AFMPHPAuthenticaionService.zip`, and `J-AMFPHPExampleServicesPlugin.zip`. You can install these from the **Extensions | Install/Uninstall** screen of the Joomla! administration area. Once installed, you will get a folder tree, as shown in the following screenshot:

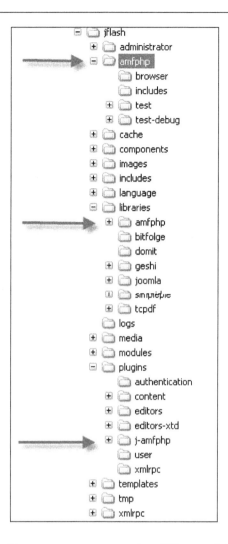

We are looking into this directory structure as it will be useful for starting the service browser.

One of the limitations of J-AMFPHP is that it lacks documentation. You cannot start using it straight after installing the component and plugins. You need some tweaking and those tweaks are really tricky to find out.

Configuring J-AMFPHP

First of all, you need to download the latest version of the AMFPHP package. You can download version 1.9 beta from `http://sourceforge.net/projects/amfphp/files`. After downloading the package, extract it somewhere onto your computer, say `e:\amfphp`. Then browse to the extracted folder, `e:\amfphp`, and copy the folder `e:\amfphp\services\amfphp` to the `plugins/j-amfphp/` folder of your Joomla! installation so that we have a `plugins/j-amfphp/amfphp` folder. Now, point your browser to the `amfphp/browser` folder on your server, for example, `http://localhost/jflash/amfphp/browser/`. This brings up the service browser with two services, as shown in the following screenshot:

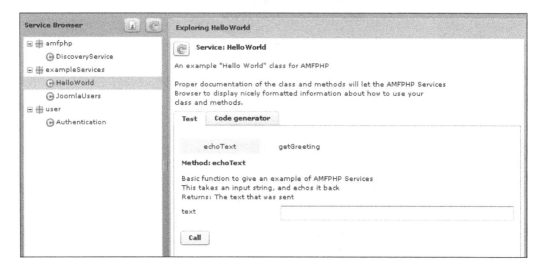

 If you don't see the above screen, or get some error messages, then please read the section on troubleshooting J-AMFPHP in Chapter 8, *Troubleshoot Your Applications*.

As you can see, the service browser lists the available services. The **HelloWorld** and **JoomlaUsers** services were installed with J-AMFPHP, whereas we have copied **DiscoveryService** with the `amfphp` folder. Selecting a service from the left pane displays the details of the service on the right pane. It has two tabs: **Test** and **Code generator**, as can be seen in the following screenshot:

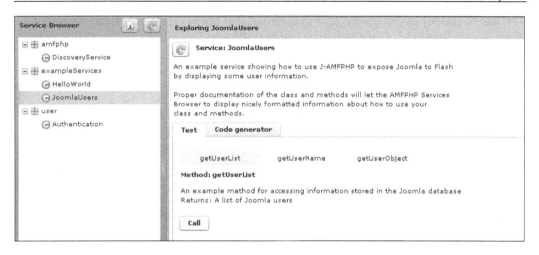

You can test the service by clicking on the **Test** tab. For example, consider that we want to test the **JoomlaUsers** service. This service is designed to get the list of Joomla! users. As you can see from the **Test** tab, it has three methods: `getUserList`, `getUserName`, and `getUserObject`. The first method, `getUserList`, takes no parameter and returns the list of users available in Joomla!. The second method, `getUserName`, takes the user ID as a parameter and returns the name of that user. The third method, `getUserObject`, also takes the user ID as a parameter and returns that user object with the associated information. For a simple test, click on the **Call** button, and you will get the list of the users in Joomla!, as shown in the following screenshot:

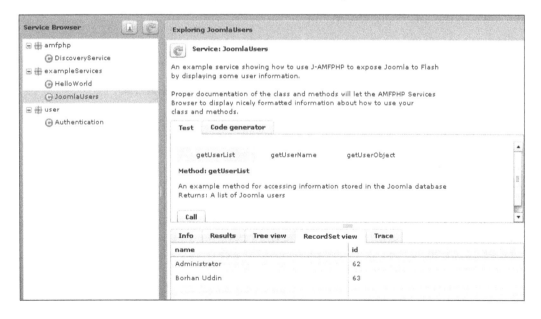

The use of the service browser is to make sure that the services you have designed work just as intended. Once you are sure that the services work, you can start using them in Flash objects.

Caution

The service browser in AMFPHP is not secure. These files should only be used in the development environment. These files should be excluded while uploading to the production server. Otherwise, this will allow anyone to view your AMF service composition, which exposes your site to security risks.

Designing services

So far, we have seen how to configure J-AMFPHP. We have also seen that the example web services work fine with J-AMFPHP. Now we will move on to see how to design such services. If you have no idea about such services, then first look into the service files `JoomlaUsers.php` and `HelloWorld.php` in the `plugins/j-amfphp` folder.

Let us design a service that will send a list of articles in Joomla!. For doing so, create a folder named `joomla_articles` within the `plugins/j-amfphp` directory. Now, create a file `JoomlaArticles.php`, and store it in the `plugins/j-amfphp/joomla_articles` folder. Now let's test what happens. Browse to `http://localhost/jflash/amfphp/browser/`. You will find the service listed, as shown in the following screenshot:

We see our service, `JoomlaArticles`, under the folder `joomla_articles`. However, clicking on it will show no method in the right pane as we have not defined the class yet. Let's open the `plugins/j-amfphp/joomla_articles/JoomlaArticles.php` file in a text editor and add the following code to it:

```
class JoomlaArticles {

  /**
  * Gets titles of articles from Joomla!
  *
  */

  function getArticleList() {
    $database = JFactory::getDBO();
    $database->setQuery( "SELECT id, title FROM #__content WHERE
                                                      state=1" );
    $results = $database->loadObjectList();
    return $results;
  }

  /**
  * Gets full article based on article id
  *
  */
  function getFullArticle ($id) {
    $database = JFactory::getDBO();
    $database->setQuery( "SELECT * FROM #__content WHERE id=$id" );
    $results = $database->loadObjectList();
    return $results;

    }

}
```

Save the file with this code and go back to the **Service Browser** screen. Click on the JoomlaArticles service, and you get the following screen with two methods listed:

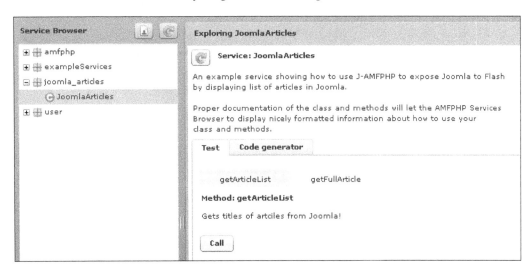

As you can see, now we have two methods, getArticleList and getFullArticle. Clicking on the method name will show the description of that method. Select the getArticleList method, and click on the **Call** button. This will list the published articles, as shown in the following screenshot:

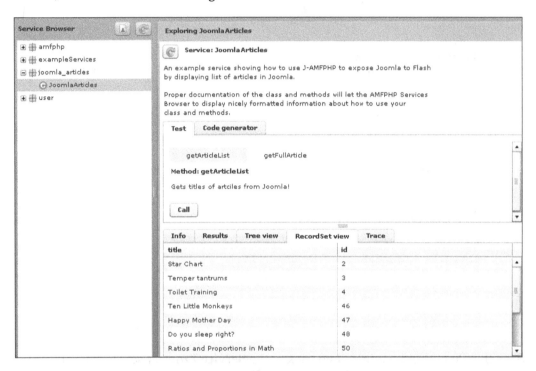

Now we want to view a complete article. For viewing a full article, we need to pass the ID of that article as a parameter to the getFullArticle() method. Consider for example, that we want to see the article named **Star Chart**, whose **id** is **2**. Now click on getFullArticle method, and you get a textbox to enter the **id**, as shown in the following screenshot:

Type 2 in the **id** field, and click on the **Call** button. This will retrieve all the fields for the article with an ID **2**, as shown in the following screenshot:

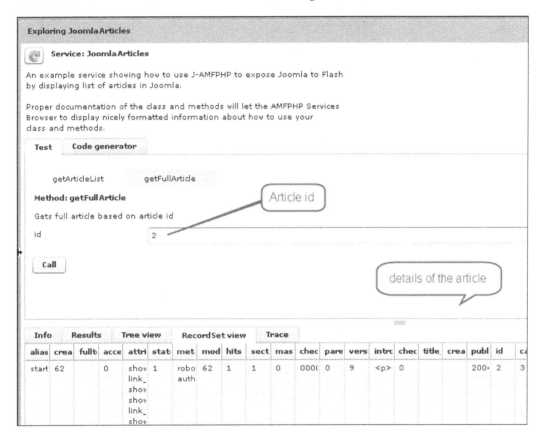

Now, we are sure that our service is working as intended. However, we need to use this data returned by our service in Flash objects. The next section describes how to consume this data into a Flash/Flex application.

Using services in Flash

Now we will see how to consume data from the web service into a Flex application. For developing the Flex application, we may use Adobe Flex Builder IDE or Flex SDK. You can download the open source Flex SDK from Adobe's site. With the help of the SDK and a text editor, you can make a Flex application that will consume the data from the web service created.

You can download a 60-day trial version of Flex Builder IDE from: `http://www.adobe.com/cfusion/entitlement/index.cfm?e=flexbuilder3`.

The design of the Flex interface in Flex3 IDE looks as shown in the following screenshot:

In fact, the above UI design is done using MXML, which can be seen by clicking on the **Source** pane. The code for this file will be as follows:

```xml
<?xml version="1.0" encoding="utf-8"?>
<mx:Application xmlns:mx="http://www.adobe.com/2006/mxml"
    layout="absolute" >

<!-- this is the RemoteObject used to make the RPC calls -->
<mx:RemoteObject id="myRemote" destination="amfphp"
    source="joomla_articles.JoomlaArticles"
    endpoint="http://localhost/jflash/amfphp/gateway.php"
    showBusyCursor="true"/>

<mx:Label text="List of Articles" width="557" enabled="true"
    fontSize="24" fontWeight="bold"    color="#0534BA" alpha="0.72"
    x="36"/>

<mx:DataGrid x="36" y="43" id="dg1" width="467"
    dataProvider="{myRemote.getArticleList.lastResult}"
    enabled="true">
```

```
    <mx:columns>
        <mx:DataGridColumn headerText="Article ID" dataField="id" />
        <mx:DataGridColumn headerText="Title" dataField="title" />
    </mx:columns>
</mx:DataGrid>

<mx:Button x="36" y="193" label="Get Data" width="133"
    id="btnGetdata" enabled="true"
    click="myRemote.getArticleList()"/>


</mx:Application>
```

As you can see, it starts with the XML declaration. The first two lines are similar for every Flex application. The crucial part is specifying the remote service through the `mx:RemoteObject` declaration. We have configured the following things with the `mx:RemoteObject` declaration:

- `id`: This is the ID that we assign to the remote object. We will be using this ID to refer to the remote object. For example, we have used it as `myRemote.getArticleList` to call the `getArticleList()` method of the remote object.

- `destination`: This is the section in the `amfphp/browser/services-config.xml` file that refers to the channel to be used. If we open the file, we find a section like the following:

```
<destination id="amfphp">
    <channels>
        <channel ref="my-amfphp"/>
    </channels>
    <properties>
        <source>*</source>
    </properties>
</destination>
```

We have referred to the ID `amfphp` in our code.

- `source`: This is the name of the remote service. It is generally expressed in the format `FolderName.ServiceName`. We have used `joomla_articles.JoomlaArticles` to indicate that the service `JoomlaArticles` resides in the `joomla_articles` folder.

- `endpoint`: The endpoint is the URI of the Flash Remoting gateway. Our gateway file resides at `http://localhost/jflash/amfphp/`. Therefore, we have put `http://localhost/jflash/amfphp/gateway.php` as the endpoint.

Later in the code, we have added the Label, DataGrid, and Button objects. The data grid object starts with the `mx:DataGrid` tag. Note that we have specified `dataProvider` as `myRemote.getArticleList.lastResult`, which will populate data from the `getArticle()` method of the `JoomlaArticles` service. In defining columns, we have bound two columns to two fields: `id` and `title`.

Finally, we have defined a button element through the `mx:Button` tag. Through its click event, we call the `getArticleList()` method of our service `JoomlaArticles`.

Let us see how this Flex application looks now. From the Flex IDE, click on run and you will see the application running. Clicking on the **Get Data** button we see the data grid populated, as shown in the following screenshot:

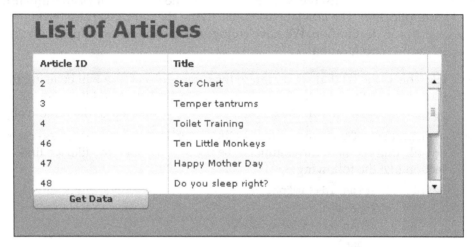

This is a simple example of using the data from a web service. With some advanced skills in Flex and ActionScript programming, you can create a full-fledged Flash/Flex website taking contents from the Joomla! database.

Ensuring accessibility of Flash content

Accessibility for websites is of high importance, especially when you are making a site for wide audiences. Joomla! as a CMS addresses the web accessibility issues by default. Using Flash objects with Joomla! may raise some accessibility issues as it is traditionally thought that Flash is less accessible for web users compared to plain HTML and other text formats. Now we are going to explore the accessibility issues with Flash and find out ways to address these issues.

Identifying accessibility issues

Flash has been used since a long time for adding interactivity to web pages. Adobe Flash is currently widely used for adding interactive items like animation, games, and so on. Although it has been used on the Web for a long time and can also be used with multiple technologies on multiple platforms, it can yet introduce some accessibility issues for individuals with disabilities.

Adobe Flash now can create highly-accessible content. However, the way it is used may always leave some groups behind in accessibility. Different concepts of HTML accessibility can also be applied to Flash, such as using appropriate contrast, understandable language, a consistent navigation, typography, and so on. More attention needs to be given to the special needs of the special groups. For example, people with hearing disabilities may benefit from synchronized captions for any audio used in conjunction with Flash movies; people with motor disabilities may prefer alternative access to the content through the keyboard; for people with blindness, presenting contents in a format ready for the screen readers will be of great help. A textual equivalent of all non-text elements will also be useful. With newer versions of Flash, all these strategies can be used to increase the accessibility. However, Flash contents are rarely used to include all of these strategies at the same time, which means that it remains inaccessible to some groups. Therefore, it is desirable that we use all the accessibility options available in Flash to make it suitable for all groups.

Addressing common accessibility issues

As indicated earlier, Adobe Flash has evolved much from its earlier days and now provides some very good accessibility features that can be used in designing accessible Flash content. Recognizing the fact that designing accessible content requires designers and developers to pay attention to the user experience, and as many developers are not familiar with capabilities of screen readers and other assistive technologies, Adobe has designed an accessibility guideline. Here are some examples suggested in the accessibility guideline to increase the accessibility of Flash content:

- Assigning text equivalents for visual elements so that screen readers can read-out the text equivalents and assist people with blindness or low vision.

- Avoiding the use of looping elements in animation to allow the screen readers to finish reading out the text equivalents instead of refreshing the same content time and again.

- Allowing the user to control the motion of animations so that they can watch and read it at their pace and the screen readers and other assistive technologies can also work properly.

- Using accessible components available in Adobe Flash, which enables the designing of accessible applications by generating appropriate labels, keyboard access keys, testing, and consistent user experience throughout the application. The `enableAccessiblity()` command in ActionScript can also be used for enabling accessibility for such components.

- Enabling control over the reading order so that users and screen readers read the content in the correct order. You can achieve this either by keeping the layout simple, by preparing a secondary linear version of the content for keeping offstage, or by specifying the reading order using ActionScript.

- Facilitating keyboard access for all the controls, making sure that the users can navigate through your movie effectively using only the keyboard.

- Providing captions to all graphic and audio elements.

- Providing accessible video controls to assist people with blindness, low-vision, and keyboard-only users.

- Enabling control over audio and video playback to facilitate the screen readers in reading out the text equivalents.

- Exposing the structure for sites and movies with complex structures so that the screen readers can read out the structure and users can go to an appropriate part as and when necessary. Either a root-level description or a separate information screen can be used for this purpose.

- Exposing the state of the controls to provide the users with feedback on the control as it changes state. For example, once a Play/Pause button is pressed, it starts playing and pressing the button again will pause the movie. Therefore, it is desirable that the state of the button is exposed to the users.

- Using colors wisely and not relying on the color alone to convey information, and ensuring sufficient contrast between the foreground and background colors for making the content easily readable.

- Validating the Flash content for accessibility to ensure that the Flash content conforms to the W3C accessibility guidelines. Direct user experience testing and various other tools can be used for such validations.

Following these strategies for making Flash content accessible will be a starting point. Adobe Flash 4 provides many accessibility features that should be used for developing accessible Flash content.

Summary

Throughout the book, we have learned how to use Flash objects within Joomla! content. But sometimes, it may be necessary to use Joomla! content in Flash. This chapter showed you how to use Joomla! content in Flash/Flex applications through web services. We have used J-AMFPHP to create web services on the Joomla! web server and consume the data from this web service into a Flex application.

Later in the chapter, we saw a brief introduction on the accessibility issues with Flash and how to address these issues. Although there are several accessibility issues with the use of Flash, these can be addressed if the Flash designers and developers are familiar with these issues. We have also briefly listed the principles of Flash accessibility in this chapter.

In the next chapter, we will be looking into the troubleshooting of applications — both with Joomla! and the components that we have used in this book.

8
Troubleshoot Your Applications

Maintenance and troubleshooting are an integral part of any application. Flash applications integrated with Joomla! may also need some troubleshooting from time-to-time. This chapter focuses on the common problems that you may face when using Flash with the Joomla! CMS. On the completion of this chapter you will be able to troubleshoot:

- Common problems with Joomla!
- Common problems with Flash
- Joomla! extensions used in this book

Troubleshooting is largely dependent on the actual environment around it. However, we will examine some of the common scenarios where you may face some problems when using Flash with Joomla!. These cases are illustrative, and you may find other kinds of problems too. The best way of finding solutions in such cases would be to consult relevant websites and forums.

Issues related to Joomla!

The best place to search for solutions for problems related to Joomla! is the Joomla! forum at `http://forum.joomla.org`. First, search the forum for the problem and its solution. If you do not find a similar problem reported, then register with the forum and post the problem to the forum. As the Joomla! community is very large, you may expect to get the solution quickly. The more descriptively and clearly you report your problem, more are the chances of getting the correct solution quickly.

The Joomla! forum has many sections, and it is convenient to browse to the relevant sections. For example, if you suspect that the problem on your Joomla! site has been caused by a particular component, then visit the **Extensions | Components** section of the Joomla! forum.

Problems with installation of extensions

In Joomla! 1.5, you can install all the extensions from one place, **Extensions | Install/Uninstall**. However, in Joomla! 1.0.x, you need to select different screens based on the type of extension you are going to install. This used to create a lot of trouble in installation of extensions as some of the administrators were installing modules from the component installation screen. Joomla! 1.5.x eliminates such confusion. However, you may still face some problems while installing extensions.

The following are some of the common errors that occur during the installation of extensions:

- You may get an error message saying that direct access to a directory is not possible. This happens mainly due to inappropriate permissions to the directory or a Joomla! installation with inappropriate access rights. You can solve this problem by setting appropriate permissions for the directory; especially the write permissions to the group in the component and template installation directories.

- For some extensions, you may be warned that the extension is written for an earlier version of Joomla!, so you will need to enable the **System - Legacy** plugin to work with it. This happens if you try to install an extension marked as '1.5 legacy mode'. You must enable the **System - Legacy** plugin from **Extensions | Plugin Manager** to run such type of extensions.

- While installing some extensions, you may be notified that another template/component/module/extension is in the same location. This happens if you have already installed the extension, or there is another extension with the same name. To solve this problem, first uninstall the previously installed extension, and then try installing it again. If you cannot uninstall the extension from the Joomla! admin area, then login to cPanel and delete the respective folder, for example ./administrator/components/com_links, from the web server.

- With some extensions you may get an error message saying that the XML setup file could not be found in the package. It may be due to the fact that the XML file is corrupt, missing, or does not exist at all. To verify the package, open the zipped package file on your local computer and check if the XML file exists with the correct name and is in the correct format. You will also get this message if you try to install an extension solely designed for Joomla! 1.0.x.

As we have seen, most of the installation problems are related to either insufficient permissions or inappropriate package files. You can avoid these easily by checking for an appropriate version of the package and ensuring that the permissions are correctly set for the directories.

For detailed information about setting file permissions, read this article at Wikipedia: http://en.wikipedia.org/wiki/File_system_permissions.

As a general rule, never set 777 (read-write access to owner, group, and others) for any file. Set 755 for folders and 644 for files. The configuration file should be protected first, therefore, once the configuration is done, set the file permission 444 for the configuration.php file.

SEF problems

Joomla! administrators often face some common errors after enabling **Search Engine Friendly URLs**. When you enable SEF from the Global Configuration screen, Joomla! generates search engine friendly URLs. However, if you choose to use mod_rewrite, the SEF may not work as expected. This may happen due to the fact that you have not renamed the file htaccess.txt to .htaccess. When you choose to use mod_rewrite, you also have to use the .htaccess file that comes with the Joomla! installation package. You may also face problems even after renaming the htaccess.txt to .htaccess. In this case you need to check the .htaccess file. First, make sure that RewriteEngine On is present in the file. Then, check for the line with RewriteBase. This line should reflect your Joomla! root directory. For example, if Joomla! is installed in the ./public_html/jflash/ directory, then the .htaccess file should contain RewriteBase ./public_html/jflash/.

SEF problems may occur due to a misconfigured .htaccess file. Sometimes you can solve SEF problems by commenting out the line with Options +FollowSymLinks in the .htaccess file. Before changing this file, you should have a clear understanding of its directives.

To configure SEF for Joomla! correctly and to solve related problems, refer to *Joomla! 1.5 SEO* published by Packt Publishing. Two other titles, *Joomla! Web Security* and *Joomla! Accessibility*, will also help you secure your site and optimize the use of the php.ini and .htaccess files.

Issues related to Flash

When using Joomla! with some Flash content, you may face problems which can be attributed to Flash. We often tend to find bugs in applications, which in fact originate from supporting technologies like Flash. This section illustrates these issues.

Flash 10 and Joomla! Flash Uploader

Many Flash-based web uploaders do not work with Flash 10. Joomla! 1.5.x has a Flash-based uploader. You can enable it by selecting **Yes** for the **Enable Flash Uploader** field in **Site | Global Configuration | System**. Once this Flash uploader is enabled, it should look as shown in the following screenshot:

First, the uploader lists the files selected for upload. You can select multiple files and upload them at the same time. When the **Start Upload** button is clicked, the files start uploading and a progress bar for each file is displayed. When the upload is finished, you will see the progress bars shown in the following screenshot:

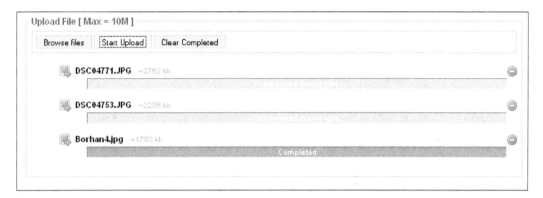

This Flash uploader may not work as shown here when you are using Flash 10. A way around this is to either downgrade your Flash Player to version 9 or disable the Flash uploader by selecting **No** in the **Enable Flash Uploader** field in **Site | Global Configuration | System**.

For removing Flash Player 10, you should follow the instructions provided at `http://kb2.adobe.com/cps/141/tn_14157.html`. It gives you an opportunity to download an uninstaller for Flash Player 10. Once uninstalled using this uninstaller, download Flash Player 9 from `http://www.adobe.com/support/flashplayer/ downloads.html` and install it. Do remember to restart your computer when prompted to do so.

Inserting a Flash object in the Joomla! header

When using Flash with Joomla!, you may need to embed some Flash code directly into templates. For example, you may want to show a Flash header in a template. The header Flash objects reside in the `./flash` folder. In general, to embed a Flash object called `header.swf`, residing in the `./flash` directory, we use the following code:

```
<param name="movie" value="flash/header.swf">
```

This locates the Flash object `header.swf` in the `flash` directory. However, this will not work in Joomla!. For Joomla!, you need to keep the Flash files in a subdirectory under the directory of the template in use and specify the path differently. The line of code will look like the following in Joomla!:

```
<object type="application/x-shockwave-flash" data="<?php echo
  $this->baseurl; ?>/templates/
<?php echo $this->template?>/flash/header.swf" width="700"
                                                height="240">
 <param name="wmode" value="transparent" />
```

```
<param name="movie" value="<?php echo $this->baseurl; ?>
 /templates/<?php echo $this->template?>/flash/header.swf" />
</object>
```

As you can see, the file path is generated dynamically and refers to the `flash` directory inside the template's folder.

Issues related to individual extensions

We have used several Joomla! extensions throughout the book. It is possible that you have had problems while configuring and using these extensions with Joomla!. Of course, not all extensions will give you trouble but some can. The following sections illustrate a few problems with some of the extensions discussed in this book. Of course there might be some other problems as well. For troubleshooting such problems their respective support forums will be of great help. The following sections will also give you addresses of the websites and support forums from where you can seek help.

Expose Flash Gallery

Installing Expose Flash Gallery may prevent the Joomla! frontend from showing anything. When you browse to the Joomla! frontend, it may show a blank page with absolutely nothing displayed not even an error message. To find out what's happening, you may try to amend error reporting in the **Global Configuration | Server | Server Settings** section, shown in the following screenshot:

Change the **Error Reporting** field from **System Default** to **Maximum** and save the configuration. Now when you browse to the Joomla! frontend, you will get the following error message:

Fatal error: Cannot redeclare domxml_new_doc() in C:\wamp\www\jflash\ components\com_expose\expose\manager\misc\domxml-php4-to-php5.php on line 41

You can see that the problem is with DOMXML. It usually happens with PHP5.x installations. One way is to turn the DOMXML extension off in the `php.ini` file. Open the `php.ini` file in a text editor and locate the following line:

```
extension=php_domxml.dll
```

Comment out the line by adding a semicolon (;) at the start of the line. Save the file, restart your web server, and browse to the Joomla! site. You will now be able to see the frontend.

> For troubleshooting with the Expose Flash Gallery, refer to the forum at http://www.gotgtek.net/forum/. The forum is quiet supportive, and you will get many other possible solutions to such problems.

YOS amChart

YOS amChart may display error messages if you are using PHP5. With YOS amChart on PHP5.x, you may get the following error message:

Warning: Call-time pass-by-reference has been deprecated in C:\wamp\www\ jflash\plugins\content\yos_amchart.php on line 15

To solve this open up the file referenced in this message and locate line 15, which contains the following line of code:

```
$arr_obj_chart = pluginChartHelper::getPattern($row, '/\{yos_amchart
                                               .*?\}/', $params);
```

Note the last word of the line, `$params`, which is causing the error. PHP4 supported passing values by reference. However, in PHP5, it becomes deprecated. You will get this error message only on a server running PHP5. One way to solve it is to delete the dollar sign ($) from `$params` and saving it. That will work fine without displaying the error message.

Another way of solving this is to edit the php.ini file. In the php.ini file, locate this line:

```
allow_call_time_pass_reference = Off
```

This line in your php.ini file causes the error message. You need to turn it on by typing On in place of Off. The line will then look as follows:

```
allow_call_time_pass_reference = On
```

In PHP5 and above versions, this is set to Off for keeping the code clean.

 There may be some other problems with YOS amChart. Fortunately, there is a good support site for YOS amChart, and you can visit it at http://www.amcharts.com/forum/.

The Random Flash Module

In the Random Flash Module for Joomla! 1.5, you just need to configure the folder path for the Flash files, and the width and the height. These are set from the **Module Parameters** section in **Module: [Edit]**. Once these are set, you will notice that Flash objects are displayed properly in Microsoft Internet Explorer and other non-Netscape browsers, but not in Mozilla Firefox and some Netscape-based browsers.

This may happen due to the support for the <object> </object> and <embed> </embed> tags. The classid attribute mentioned in the <object> tag is ActiveX specific. That's why it doesn't get displayed even in some IE browsers.

To solve this problem, open the module file `./modules/mod_j15randomflash/mod_j15randomflash.php` in your text editor, and before the closing `</object>` tag, add the following line:

```
<embed type="application/x-shockwave-flash" width="$width"
      height="$height" src="$flashbase/$top.swf">
</embed>
```

Now the code for embedding Flash looks change to as follows:

```
$content = <<<EOD
<object classid="clsid:d27cdb6e-ae6d-11cf-96b8-444553540000"
        codebase="http://fpdownload.macromedia.com/pub/shockwave/
                  cabs/flash/swflash.cab#version=7,0,0,0"
  width="$width" height="$height" id="g1">
 <param name="movie" value="$flashbase/$top.swf"/>
 <param name="loop" value="true"/>
 <param name="quality" value="$quality"/>
 <param name="bgcolor" value="$background"/>
 <embed type="application/x-shockwave-flash" width="$width"
        height="$height" src="$flashbase/$top.swf"></embed>
</object>
EOD;
```

Having changed the code as highlighted, save the file and browse to the site's frontend. You will see Flash objects displayed both in IE as well as Firefox.

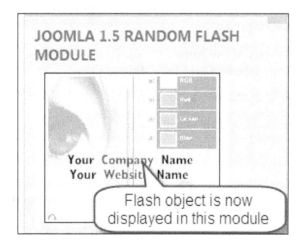

For more troubleshooting information on Joomla! 1.5 Random FlashModule, visit its support forum at http://www.dart-creations.com/forums.

Ozio Gallery

Ozio Gallery has lots of configuration options. If a specific configuration is not working, then recheck the configuration and read the instructions given inline once again. You can also get help from its support site at http://forum.joomla.it/index.php/board,73.0.html.

Dynamic Flash Gallery

Dynamic Flash Gallery displays the gallery using inline frames. For security, inline frames are discouraged, and some browsers do not show content in inline frames. This component will not work unless your browser supports inline frames.

JVideo!

The JVideo! component for Joomla! is well documented. Whenever a problem arises, first consult the documentation at http://jvideo.infinovision.com/support/user-guide and then, its support forum http://jvideo.infinovision.com/support/forum. Most of the problems submitted to the forum are answered, and you can expect a quick response.

The plugin for JVideo! may show some notices. To prevent these warnings, you need to edit the php.ini file, and add the following line:

```
error_reporting = E_ALL & ~E_NOTICE
```

This will show all errors except for warnings and coding standards.

Another problem with JVideo! is that you may get stuck with a message like the following:

Warning: DOMDocument::loadXML() [function.DOMDocument-loadXML]: Start tag expected, '<' not found in Entity, line: 1 in /home/suhreed/public_html/jflash/components/com_jvideo/ assets/lib/infin-lib.php on line 96

Fatal error: Call to a member function getAttribute() on a non-object in /home/suhreed/public_html/jflash/components/ com_jvideo/assets/lib/infin-lib.php on line 99

This may happen when your server is using libxml2 2.7.2. The bug exists in libxml2 2.7.2, which strips off the braces when parsing XML files. To solve this problem you need to downgrade libxml2 2.7.2 to its earlier versions, say libxml2 2.6.x. Your hosting provider may help you in this regard.

J-AMFPHP

Configuring and running J-AMFPHP is easy when you know the tricks. After downloading and installing the J-AMFPHP package, you will have no clue about where to start from. It will not even tell you that it requires you to download the latest version of the AMFPHP package. Even downloading the AMFPHP package may cause a severe problem. You need to visit its website www.amfphp.org and download the AMFPHP package from SourceForge.net, using the link provided on the home page. The SourceForge.net page lists many versions of the AMFPHP package, where amfphp-1.9.beta.20080120.zip is the latest.

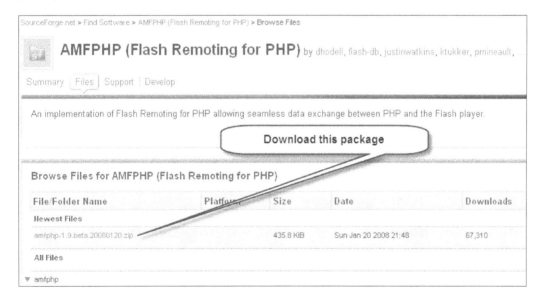

You may prefer to download the stable version rather than the beta, which is ampfphp 1.0.1. Doing this and extracting the files in the J-AMFPHP folders, as per the instructions given in Chapter 7, will lead you to lots of trouble. First, with the default installation of J-AMFPHP, when you browse to the service browser, you get an error message like the one shown in the following screenshot:

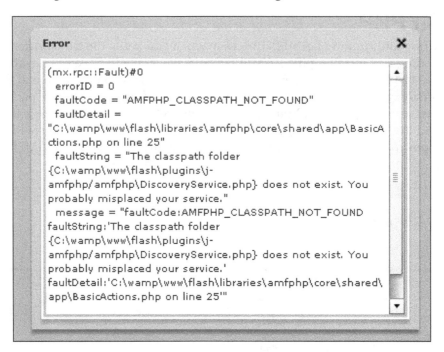

To get rid of this message, you must download version 1.9 beta from http://sourceforge.net/projects/amfphp/files. After downloading the package, extract it on your computer, say in the e:\amfphp directory. Then, copy the e:\amfphp\services\amfphp folder to the plugins/j-amfphp/ folder of your Joomla! installation. Now point your browser to the amfphp/browser folder on your server, for example, http://localhost/flash/amfphp/browser/. This shows the available services.

If you download other versions, with the exception of version 1.9 beta, you may get error messages like the ones shown in the following screenshot:

Although beta versions are often not recommended for use, J-AMFPHP is built upon the AMFPHP 1.9 beta version. Therefore, you must use this version and copy the required files into the J-AMFPHP installation folders, as instructed in Chapter 7.

Summary

Maintenance and troubleshooting are an integral part of any application. At any stage of the application—installation, configuration, and use—a problem may occur. As the applications covered in this book are open source and distributed free of cost, it is often difficult to get enough documentation for solving such problems. This chapter focused on some of the key issues related to Joomla!, Flash, and the individual extensions, which may arise during the exercises depicted in this book. Besides pointing to the probable solution for such problems, we have referred to relevant websites and forums from where you can get more help to solve problems.

Resources for Joomla! and Flash

The main text of the book referred to many Joomla! extensions, and we have learned how to use those extensions for using Flash with the Joomla! CMS. This appendix gives you a list of some more resources that can be useful when using Flash with Joomla!. First it shows you some resources for Joomla!, and then, Flash extension-specific resources.

Resources for Joomla!

As indicated earlier, there are hundreds of sites providing resources for Joomla!. With the increasing popularity of Joomla!, new sites are coming into operation and which provide new services. The following are some of the sites you should search for Joomla! resources:

- **Joomla! Home page** (http://www.joomla.org): This is the first place you should check when searching for resources for Joomla!. This site provides updates on Joomla! development and the news relevant to Joomla!. This also serves as an entry point to Joomla! Extensions Directory, the download site, the support site, and the documentation site.

- **Joomla! Forum** (http://forum.joomla.org): The Joomla! forum is an indispensable resource for any Joomla! site builder. If you find a problem on your site and suspect that it might be related to Joomla!, search the forum first. The forum is divided into several sections.

- **Joomla! Extensions Directory** (http://extensions.joomla.org): Many of the extensions mentioned in this book are available at the Joomla! Extensions Directory. Check this directory regularly to find updates for the extensions that you are using for your site.

- **JoomlaCode** (http://joomlacode.org): This is a software repository for Joomla!. Developers can build and host their Joomla! extensions on this server. Almost all of the popular Joomla! extensions can be found here. The extensions listed in the Joomla! Extensions Directory are often downloaded from the joomlacode.org server.

- **Joomla! Documentation** (http://docs.joomla.org): This is the Joomla! official documentation site. Start reading the available documents on this site before you start building your first Joomla! site.

- **Joomla! Developer Site** (http://developer.joomla.org): This site is for Joomla! developers. If you are interested in learning more about Joomla! development and want to join the Joomla! developer team, then this is the best place to start.

- **Best of Joomla** (http://www.bestofjoomla.com): This site can be a good place to look for Joomla! templates, extensions, and other resources. This site aggregates information from other Joomla! sites and provides categorized listings of templates, extensions, and tutorials.

- **Joomla Tutorials** (http://www.joomlatutorials.com): This site provides useful tutorials for building Joomla!-based web sites. The video tutorials section can be of great help to beginners.

- **Joomla24** (http://www.joomla24.com): This is a vast database where you can search for free Joomla! templates.

- **Joom!Fish** (www.joomfish.net): This is the home page for the Joom!Fish extension. It has an updated documentation and an active forum. Refer to these when you face problems with multilingual content created with Joom!Fish.

- **extensions.Siliana.com** (http://extensions.siliana.com): You can obtain the sh404sef extension from this website. Visit this site for the latest release of sh404sef. Refer to the forum if you have any problem with the extension.

There are many other sites for Joomla! that can help you find specific information on a topic. The best way is to search the Internet for the information you want on Joomla!.

Resources for Flash

If you search for Flash on the web, you will get a lot of information as Flash has been around since a long time. However, you may find only little of this information useful when using Flash with Joomla!. The following extensions will help you when using Flash with the Joomla! CMS:

- **Joomla Random Flash Module**: This module shows images or Flash movies from a folder on a Joomla! web site. This module has two versions, one for Joomla! 1.0.x and another for Joomla! 1.5.x. You can download both for free, but you need to register on their site. For more information on this module, visit `http://www.dart-creations.com/Joomla/Joomla-Modules/Joomla-Random-Flash-Module.html`.

- **The Flash Module**: The Flash Module displays Flash movies (`.swf` files) in a Joomla! module. It uses parameters to control some of the Flash Player settings. This module is available for both Joomla! 1.0.x and Joomla! 1.5.x. For details of this module, visit `http://extensions.joomla.org/extensions/core-enhancements/flash-management/366`. To download the latest version, visit `http://joomlacode.org/gf/project/flashmod/frs/`.

- **Flash Module**: This module is suitable for publishing a Flash movie using a Joomla! module. It is designed for Joomla! 1.0.x but works in Joomla! 1.5.x in the legacy mode. For details of this module and downloading it, visit `http://www.futuron-web.net/downloads/flash-module-for-joomla.html`.

- **yOpensource**: yOpenSource provides the YOS amCharts and YOS amMap Joomla! components. For information and tutorials on these two components, visit their site at `http://yopensource.com/`.

- **Expose Flash Gallery**: You can download Expose Flash Gallery for Joomla! from `http://joomlacode.org/gf/project/expose/frs/`. It has all the files listed for downloading the Joomla! components, modules, and plugins. Select the latest versions while downloading. You can get support for Expose Flash Gallery at their support forum `http://www.gotgtek.net/forum/`.

- **YOS amChart**: Details about YOS amChart can be found at `http://yopensource.com/en/joomla-extensions/24-financial-and-statistics/42-yos-amchart-graphs-and-charts-solutions-for-joomla-15x`. This page describes the features of YOS amChart and also contains a download link. You can purchase the pro version from here. The page also contains examples for the same. The documentation for YOS amChart is available at `http://yopensource.com/en/documentation/yos-amchart`.

- **YOS amMap**: Information about YOS amMap is available at `http://yopensource.com/en/joomla-extensions/25-images-and-multimedia/22-yos-ammap-map-tool-solutions-for-joomla-15x`. You will find feature lists and download link along with some examples. The documentation for YOS amMap is available at `http://yopensource.com/en/documentation/yos-ammap`.

- **The Random Flash Module**: Joomla! Random Flash Module can display Flash movies randomly from a directory. You can get details of this module and download it from `http://www.dart-creations.com/Joomla/Joomla-Modules/Joomla-Random-Flash-Module.html`. The module is freely available for both Joomla! 1.0.x and Joomla! 1.5.x, but you need to register to their site before downloading the module.

- **Simple Video Flash Player**: The Simple Video Flash Player module can play Flash-based videos on a Joomla! site. You can download this module from `http://www.joomlaos.de/Joomla_CMS_Downloads/Joomla_Module/Simple_Video_Flash_Player.html`. You can get the feature list and the documentation about it at `http://www.time2online.de/joomla-extensions`.

- **AllVideos for Joomla!**: The AllVideos plugin for Joomla! can be used to play Flash videos in Joomla!. You can get details about this plugin at `http://www.joomlaworks.gr/content/view/16/42/`. The documentation for this plugin is available at `http://www.joomlaworks.gr/content/view/35/41/`.

- **Flash Floating Menu**: The Flash Floating Menu module can be downloaded from `http://www.myjoomlaplace.com/downloads.html`. There are versions available for Joomla! 1.0.x as well as Joomla! 1.5.x.

- **Web Flash Module for Joomla! 1.5**: Web Flash Module for Joomla! is a commercially-licensed module that can be used as the header, banner, menu, and an image gallery. You can find details about the module and download a demo version from `http://www.webpsilon.com/joomla-extensions/index.php?option=com_content&view=article&id=13&Itemid=8`.

- **Ozio Gallery**: Ozio Gallery is a photo gallery for Joomla! with 3D Flash animation. You can download this component from `http://www.joomla.it/download/oziogallery.html`. It has a support forum at `http://forum.joomla.it/index.php/board,73.0.html`.

- **Simple Flash Image Gallery (SFIG)**: Simple Flash Image Gallery is a Flash-based image gallery for Joomla!. You can download this component from `http://www.webmaster-tips.net/Joomla-1.0-and-1.5/Joomla-1.5-Components-/Simple-Flash-Image-Gallery-J1.5-SFIG.html`.

- **Dynamic Flash Gallery**: Dynamic Flash Gallery is a Flash-based image gallery with a slideshow effect. The details of this component are available at `http://www.webmaster-tips.net/joomla-component-dynamic-flash-image-gallery-v-2.html`.

- **sIFR**: You can display non-web fonts in Joomla! using the sIFR plugin available at `http://www.joomla-addons.org/option,com_docman/task,cat_view/gid,27/Itemid,152.html`.

- **Flash Uploader**: Joomla! Flash Uploader is a Flash-based uploader. It is available at `http://www.tinywebgallery.com/en/tfu/web_jfu.php` as a component as well as a plugin.

- **JVideo**: JVideo is a Joomla! video component, available for download at `http://jvideo.infinovision.com/download`. Besides the main component for JVideo, it has several plugins for using it as a gallery, inside content, and for enabling video searching. It can also work with JomSocial, Community Builder, and JoomlaComment with the use of appropriate plugins.

- **Simple MP3 Bar**: Simple MP3 bar is a Flash-based MP3 player for Joomla!. It is available for download at `http://www.box.net/shared/7c0xrun7oj`.

- **Unmp3 for Joomla! 1.5**: Unmp3 is an MP3 player for Joomla! 1.5.x. You can download it from `http://www.unmp3.com/unmp3_download.html`. The detail documentation is available at `http://www.unmp3.com/joomla_mp3_player_free.html`.

- **Flash MP3 Player**: Flash MP3 Player is a customizable Flash-based MP3 player for Joomla!. This commercially licensed module is available at `http://www.myjoomlaplace.com/joomla-15-extensions/modules/35-joomla-15-modules/68-joomla-15-flash-mp3-player.html`.

- **Joom!FreeMind**: Joom!FreeMind is a visual mind-mapping component for Joomla! that can track the Joomla! menus, sections, and categories and build a visual sitemap. This is available for download at `http://www.dcos.ro/joomfreemind/doc_details/22-joomfreemind-v225.html`. The documentation for this extension is available at `http://www.dcos.ro/en/current-projects/joomfreemind.html`.

- **J-AMFPHP**: J-AMFPHP is a library for Joomla! based on AMFPHP, which enables Flash Remoting in Joomla!. This can be downloaded from `http://joomlacode.org/gf/project/jamfphp/frs/`.

As you can see, we have only mentioned those available extensions for Joomla! which can help you in using Flash with Joomla!. There are many other extensions like these. You can search the Internet to find out new resources that can help you in using Flash with Joomla!.

Summary

There are many resources for Joomla! and Flash available on the Web. In this Appendix, we have listed the ones that we have used in this book. Of course this is not a comprehensive list and there are many other relevant resources may be outside of this list. Therefore, it is recommended to search the Internet regularly for new and updated resources for Joomla! and Flash.

Index

Symbols

3D bar chart, Open Flash Chart 14

A

Accordion skin
  about 101
  settings, configuring 101
ActionScript libraries
  about 15
  ActionScript.org Library 15
  ActionScript Physics Engine 15
  Senocular.com ActionScript Library 15
ActionScript.org Library 15
ActionScript Physics Engine 15
Adobe Flash 9
Adobe Flash Player
  URL 9
advanced parameters section, Flash Module
  Display using JavaScript? 36
  No Flash HTML 36
  NOSCRIPT Display 36
Ajax Animator
  about 11
  downloading 11
  interface 11
album manager, Expose Flash Gallery 71
AllVideos for Joomla! 232
amCharts
  about 13
  data file 138-140
  settings file 135-138
AMF 200
AMFPHP 200

AMFPHP package
  downloading 202
Animated Charts 13
Apache web server 17

B

Best of Joomla 230

C

Carousel skin
  about 104
  settings, configuring 104, 105
chart
  amChart, data file 138, 140
  amChart, settings file 135-138
  creating 134, 135
  embedding in content, plugin used 147, 148
  publishing, module used 140-147
Combo Ken Burns Effects, transition type
    field 28
configuration, Expose Flash Gallery
  about 68
  font settings 70
  gallery settings, defining 69
  main settings 68

D

database server 17
development environment
  example website 20
  PHP 18
  setting up 17
  web server 17

T

The Flash Module 231
Tilt 3D skin
  about 93
  settings, configuring 93-96
transition type field, RokSlideShow
troubleshooting
  Flash, issues related to 218
  individual extensions, issues related to 220
  Joomla!, issues related to 215

U

UnMP3 169-172
Unmp3, for Joomla! 1.5 233

V

video, embedding
  plugin used 45

W

Web Flash Module
  downloading 60
  for Joomla! 1.5 60-65
  parameters section 61, 63
  using, to show headers 196
Web Flash Module for Joomla! 1.5 232
Web Flash Module, parameters section
  % Menu Button Height 62
  background color 62
  Border 62
  border color 62
  Button Style 63
  Button Text align 63
  Buttons background color, separated by
    intros 63
  Buttons text color, separated by intros 63
  Buttons Width autoscale 62
  Images Animation 62
  Images Folder 61
  Images in the buttons? 63
  Images transition effect 62
  Images transition time in seconds 62
  Manual buttons Links separated by
    intros 63

  Manual texts buttons separated by intros
    64
  Menu Button Separation 63
  Menu Button Width 63
  Menu Font Size 62
  Menu Name 61
  Menu Style 61
  Menu text font 63
  Module height 62
  Module width, number with px or % 62
  Number 0-100 62
  number with px 62
  target link 62
  Text in button if button is parent 63
Wink
  downloading 12
  features 13
  interface 12, 13
wiping, transition type field 28

Y

yOpensource 231
YOS amChart
  amChart, data file 138-140
  amChart, settings file 135-138
  chart, creating 134, 135
  chart embedding in content, plugin used
    147, 148
  configuring 133
  issues 221, 222
  publishing, module used 140-147
  used, for displaying charts 133
YOS amMap
  downloading 118
  installing 118-120
  map, creating 121, 122
  map data file 122-126
  map files, adding 120
  map, publishing through module 127-130
  map settings file 126, 127
  map showing in content, plugin
    used 130-132
  used, for displaying map 118

Z

zooming, transition type field 28

Thank you for buying
Joomla! With Flash

Packt Open Source Project Royalties

When we sell a book written on an Open Source project, we pay a royalty directly to that project. Therefore by purchasing Joomla! With Flash, Packt will have given some of the money received to the Joomla! project.

In the long term, we see ourselves and you—customers and readers of our books—as part of the Open Source ecosystem, providing sustainable revenue for the projects we publish on. Our aim at Packt is to establish publishing royalties as an essential part of the service and support a business model that sustains Open Source.

If you're working with an Open Source project that you would like us to publish on, and subsequently pay royalties to, please get in touch with us.

Writing for Packt

We welcome all inquiries from people who are interested in authoring. Book proposals should be sent to author@packtpub.com. If your book idea is still at an early stage and you would like to discuss it first before writing a formal book proposal, contact us; one of our commissioning editors will get in touch with you.

We're not just looking for published authors; if you have strong technical skills but no writing experience, our experienced editors can help you develop a writing career, or simply get some additional reward for your expertise.

About Packt Publishing

Packt, pronounced 'packed', published its first book "Mastering phpMyAdmin for Effective MySQL Management" in April 2004 and subsequently continued to specialize in publishing highly focused books on specific technologies and solutions.

Our books and publications share the experiences of your fellow IT professionals in adapting and customizing today's systems, applications, and frameworks. Our solution-based books give you the knowledge and power to customize the software and technologies you're using to get the job done. Packt books are more specific and less general than the IT books you have seen in the past. Our unique business model allows us to bring you more focused information, giving you more of what you need to know, and less of what you don't.

Packt is a modern, yet unique publishing company, which focuses on producing quality, cutting-edge books for communities of developers, administrators, and newbies alike. For more information, please visit our website: www.PacktPub.com.

PACKT
PUBLISHING

Flex 3 with Java

ISBN: 978-1-847195-34-0 Paperback: 304 pages

Develop rich internet applications quickly and easily using Adobe Flex 3, ActionScript 3.0 and integrate with a Java backend using BlazeDS 3.2

1. A step-by-step tutorial for developing web applications using Flex 3, ActionScript 3.0, BlazeDS 3.2, and Java

2. Build efficient and seamless data-rich interactive applications in Flex using a combination of MXML and ActionScript 3.0

3. Create custom UIs, Components, Events, and Item Renders to develop user friendly applications

Flash with Drupal

ISBN: 978-1-847197-58-0 Paperback: 303 pages

Build dynamic, content-rich Flash CS3 and CS4 applications for Drupal 6

1. Learn to integrate Flash applications with Drupal CMS

2. Explore a new approach where Flash and HTML components are intermixed to provide a hybrid Flash-Drupal architecture

3. Build a custom audio and video player in Flash and link it to Drupal

Please check **www.PacktPub.com** for information on our titles

www.ingramcontent.com/pod-product-compliance
Lightning Source LLC
Chambersburg PA
CBHW060537060326
40690CB00017B/3518